I0693689

<u>Cover Image.</u>

Miner at Freeze Fork, West Virginia

Transfer; United States. Office of War Information. Overseas Picture Division. Washington Division; 1944. Freeze Fork, Lot 1722, Ben Shahn

Date: 01/01/1935

Location: Freeze Fork

Source: Library of Congress

For information, see U.S. Farm Security Administration/Office of War Information Black & White Photographs http://www.loc.gov/rr/print/res/071_fsab.html

Background image: Electric Cadillac Lyriq

CHANCE SCOUT

Contents

Chapter 1

Losing Is Bad, But Never Learning From That Loss Is Much Worse.

To many voters, Democrats are weak, scared, and won't fight. That's a big part of why they lost the 2024 election to a six-times bankrupt, degenerate con man.

It's also little understood by liberals how exceedingly poorly informed, yet exceptionally self-interested, many non-Democratic voters are. Knowing this is the secret to winning enough of them over while also energizing and enthusing the Democratic base.

Part of it will have to do with stories and feelings, and part with good old-fashioned help. We will employ a technique that every salesperson and every adroit politician knows: people have to like you before they will trust you.

Through the chapters, I hope to take you on a breathtaking journey that will show you how to turn dreams into reality, and how it won't be done with a wonkish PowerPoint or by berating people.

As a critical thinker, I never punch down. I understand that the powerful need to divide normal people in order to keep stealing all the wealth. So, don't expect to hear a word from me about Democratic Party woes being caused by 'woke,' DEI, or transgender folks. Instead, I'll show how we don't have to sell out our own voters in order to win over new ones, especially younger men.

Before the end of your spellbinding odyssey, you will hold the key to getting red-state GOP voters to love both Democrats and the government. You may think this sounds insane; after all, don't millions of those voters think these two are coming to ban their Bibles, confiscate their guns, and groom their kids?

It's true, many are lost, but not all, and the persuadable need hope, delivered by people who they see fighting for them. From that wellspring of hope, we will have the kickstarter for every policy we ever wanted to enact.

There is no secret to making America great; just help people, whether with a $15 minimum wage, Medicare for All, paid sick leave, paid family leave, climate rescue policies, abortion rights, gun safety legislation, voting rights, or police reform.

The liberals' dilemma is that the GOP is very well versed in explaining how progressive social policies are 'woke' or 'cultural Marxism' and how reformist economic policies are the 'socialism' that will bankrupt America. Up to now, no one has had the key that unlocks the door behind which lies the solution to fighting that BS. Here, you will receive the key.

I'm not exaggerating when I tell you we can finally crush the GOP's tactic of dividing working folks along racial lines. Also, your head will spin when you see how easy it is to erase Americans' fear of that word 'socialism' in order to get those progressive policies passed. And once citizens see how wonderful their lives can be, expect to see Trump voters ditching their red caps to demand that we tax the rich.

Buckle up, for it's going to be a wild ride. When it's over, expect to be armed with enough simple, workable solutions that, come 2028, could win over voters in states that should be unimaginable for Democrats, like Florida and Texas, and consign Trump and MAGA—which I sometimes describe as the Confederate Taliban—and their cruel carnival of chaos to the scrapheap of history.

Chapter 2

The Democratic Messenger Who May Never Have Met A Real Voter.

After the 2024 election, many political consultants and pundits tried to explain what happened. However, there is no mystery. Trump won because over six million 2020 Democratic voters couldn't or didn't vote. Notwithstanding that, the media offered a narrative of a decisive victory. That's total BS. Out of around 152 million votes across the nation, just three states decided the election—Michigan, Pennsylvania, and Wisconsin. Trump's 230,000 extra votes over Kamala Harris in those states meant forty-four electoral college votes, which meant victory[1].

On a related note, I recall the seemingly curious conundrum of thousands of voters in New York's 14th Congressional District choosing representative Alexandria Ocasio-Cortez for Congress and Trump for the presidency in 2024. When asked why, one replied that they both 'cared' for the working class[2]. Leaving aside what an astounding con man Trump is, it brings us to the seemingly intractable paradox of why many people like Democratic policies yet hate Democrats. It's a notion that escapes liberals, but for many citizens, voting is about feelings more than it is facts, and everyone wants to feel that someone has their back. Allow me to present you with a story that might illustrate the point;

Think of Democrats as a smart but meek kid with a $20 bill who, at the school fair on a scorching hot summer's day, quietly offers to buy his classmates ice-cold smoothies. However, he calls them 'nutritionally balanced appetizing beverages' and speaks so softly that no one hears him except the rich, entitled Republican bully, who, in plain view and with the acquiescence of the teacher (corporate news media), steals the weak Dem kids $20 and yells out to his thirsty classmates, 'Ice-Cold Smoothies On Me!'. While the class is enjoying their smoothies, the Republican bully tells them the Dem kid could have done this, but because he hates them, he deliberately wanted to keep them thirsty. And as this whole sorry saga unfolds, the meek Dem kid is just standing there, soft and quiet, never bothering to remonstrate with the teacher or to correct his classmates' misconceptions by telling them it was actually *his* idea and it was *his* money that the Republican bully stole to buy the smoothies.

Alongside never shouting about their achievements, the other reason Democrats lose, not only their own voters but also find it so hard to win over enough of the other side, is that they won't fight. To explain this fatal political misunderstanding; when we're in trouble, instinctively, we want someone to step in and stand up for us. This is a primal feeling because it's about our own survival. Even if our 'hero' gets punched in the face and knocked down, their willingness to fight for us is enough to make us love them.

That courage and integrity required to make a sacrifice by fighting for other people might be the most attractive and magnetic quality a person can possess. Indeed, the willingness to punch up at power in fighting for ordinary people is part of the reason politicians like Alexandria Ocasio-Cortez and Bernie Sanders are so popular.

On a grander scale, it's the essence of why firefighters and the military are so respected. Think back to the morning of September 11th, 2001, and the images of the firefighters entering the burning World Trade Center buildings to rescue people. Or, after the terrorist attack of January 6th, 2021, to the images of the National Guardsmen protecting the seat of our democracy in Washington. On both these occasions, they were the people heading towards danger to risk themselves to protect others.

Heroism and sacrifice are points not lost on our friends in Hollywood. In the 1950s, it may have been High Noon or Bad Day at Black Rock. In modern times, we have the enormously successful Marvel and DC Studios superhero movies like Black Widow, Captain America, and Superman. Regardless of the era, the reason for these movies' popularity was that the hero was always battling to protect the 'little guy' from a powerful enemy.

"No one fucks with a Biden". Those were the words of President Biden, captured on a 'hot-mic,' spoken whilst visiting Florida in 2022.[3] He was speaking privately about the far right using the media to attack his son, Hunter, but it showed genuine emotion and fight.

The idiotic corporate media feigned shock at hearing a word I use a hundred times a day as an adverb, adjective, expletive, noun, pronoun, and verb. Hell, it's used on almost every show and movie I watch and every podcast I listen to. If the word 'fuck' concerns you more than the word 'fascism', then may I gently suggest this isn't the battle for you.

Just to the point of his words, as ever, the corporate media misinformed us by missing the point, which was that by saying it, the President sounded tough and decisive, just like a Commander-in-Chief should.

I recall another occasion when Joe turned up the heat on the media. For the whole of 2023, their pundits had been repeating Republican lies by predicting a recession. Yet, every month, the economic statistics revealed strong retail sales, manufacturing, and jobs growth[4].

By December 2023, after announcing more record low unemployment figures, Biden had reached his limit and said, "All good. Take a look. Start reporting it the right way."[5]

You will read in chapter six about how the mainstream media never carries good-news because fear is so much better for ratings; however, ever since that date, talk of recession more or less ended. That's what happens when you stand up for yourself.

History will record Joe Biden as both a phenomenal political operator in the legislative sphere and, despite the catastrophic miscalculation of his unyielding military support for Israel, as a decent man. However, his politics came from an age of decorum and consensus and, as such, he didn't understand the age he was living in, where the other side just wanted to dominate and control.

Unlike many in the political media, I won't castigate President Biden. Instead, look at Washington, where there are over two hundred and fifty Democrats in Congress, together with a whole political operative class of thousands. Yet, only about fifty of them fight hard. The vast majority won't fight, which makes them look scared and weak. So, for many voters, Democrat is a synonym for 'weak'. I agree, even though I don't want them to be.

At this juncture, I have to note that, with just over one hundred days of campaigning before the 2024 presidential election, Vice President Kamala Harris, together with her VP pick, Minnesota Governor Tim Walz, started doing something that Democrats wouldn't do by fighting. The hopeful and empathetic Harris/Walz ticket promised voters it would take on the Republican Party's fascist Project 2025 agenda, protect women's rights, have Medicare pay for sick Americans' home help[6], and guarantee the down payments for first-time home buyers.

Despite milquetoast billionaire-friendly Democratic consultants actively toning down the campaign's hopeful messaging[7], and even with the VP courting centrist billionaires like Mark Cuban, and former rabid right-wingers like Liz Cheney, this should have led to 2020 levels of voters turning out to vote[8]. But it didn't, with many potential Democratic voters either abstaining, voting third party, or even casting their ballots for a wealthy white male felon, sexual abuser, and traitor instead of a battle-tested, empathetic biracial female candidate.

Some of them were Arab-Americans and progressive young voters, furious at the Biden administration's de facto sanctioning of the Israeli government's genocidal war on Palestine, yet too naïve to see that Trump would be one thousand times worse for the Palestinians[9]. Others were the 42% of Latinos who voted for the Grand Old Party (GOP), too blind to see that MAGA Republicans see all brown folks as deportable[10]. Then there were the Teamsters and the Longshoremen's unions, who wouldn't endorse the Harris campaign even while Trump and Elon Musk laughed at stripping workers of their rights[11].

Most astonishing of all though, were the 18-29-year-old women of Gen Z. Given how Republicans had helpfully signposted a horrific Handmaid's Tale future of rape and patriarchal domination, one might have assumed that self-interest would bring them out to vote Democratic. No such luck. Six out of ten young women sat at home, and of those who bothered to vote, four out of ten went for Trump[12].

By December 2024, with Project 2025 fully revealed and the federal government set for the chopping block, reports abounded of Trump voters crying at the prospect of losing their jobs or entitlements[13]. For these people, the expression 'I never thought the leopards would eat my face'[14] was a perfect summation of their childlike mindset. 'Fuck around and find out' was a cruder, yet equally apt observation.

Perhaps the least covered yet most devastatingly effective weapon that Republicans possessed was the complicit and compliant corporate news, print, and television media, specifically the political press and pundits. These conniving and cowardly jackals spent the entire Biden presidency demeaning the president's mental competence and achievements whilst 'sanewashing' Trump and Republicans[15]. Instead of chasing down GOP lies and asking follow-up questions, these lazy corporate hacks acted as stenographers rather than journalists by regurgitating en masse the disinformation spewing out of the right-wing ecosphere, whether from Fox News or the toxic social media platforms of billionaire oligarchs Elon Musk and Mark Zuckerberg.

This being so, Trump and his circus of frenzied, fragile political freaks do put on a good 'show' of fighting. In my book, 'The Confederate Taliban,' I describe who he is 'fighting' for: his coalition of scared, fake-Christian, angry, rich, and insane voters.

Most GOP voters don't or won't see that Trump's number one interest is himself and his billionaire cronies. Still, Republicans 'confidence' has the effect of fooling both the corporate media and many normal, low-information voters that this orange creep and his toxic goons are 'competent,' 'decisive,' and 'fighting for them.'

You may have heard the expression 'It's better to beg forgiveness than ask permission.' Democrats always ask permission, and it looks so damn submissive.

> 'Please let women control their own bodies. Please ban kid-killing AR-15s. Please, can we have fair voting? Please, can the Supreme Court be nice? Please, don't murder the planet. Please, please, please.

For Republicans, saying 'NO!' to compliant, placid, and timid Democrats will always make them look tough and decisive in the eyes of the corporate media and millions of low-information voters.

Despite this, for many elite liberals, there is exasperation at the average voter for not being able to see what an existential threat to democracy the GOP has become. Indeed, coming into the election, I'm sure many of those citizens were more familiar with Project Gotham (a video game), or Project Runway (a TV show), than with Project 2025.

The fact that over half of Americans have the literacy skills of a 6th grader doesn't help[16]. That aside, most people spend their time working just to live and look after their families. Then, when they take in political information, they may get misinformed by Facebook, disinformed by Twitter, or only marginally better, watch 'The News,' with its both-sides, horse-race method of reporting politics. So, whilst voters should shoulder some of the burden of their bad decisions, a lot of our ire must land on liberal politicians who won't effectively message their own ideas.

To the point of how many people like Democratic policies, the proposed offerings in Joe Biden's original $3 trillion Build Back Better plan (that would become the Inflation Reduction Act of 2022) were all highly popular. Three months of paid family leave and three months of paid sick leave have 84% popularity[17]. The $15 minimum wage is popular with 62% of Americans[18]. Medicare for All is 57% popular (explain it better, and the figure will soar.)[19] And 79% of voters support free childcare for low-income and middle-class families. In the chapter "How to Win Every Election," I will show you how to get these policies across the line. For now, there are three big issues where the GOP beat Democrats: the economy, defense, and law and order.

We can start with the $29 trillion US economy. Telling the average American about trillions, GDP growth, or that the Dow Jones hit a record high is meaningless.

For a regular person, the economy is how they earn their money and what goods cost. For a baker, the 'economy' is how easy it is to find customers who will pay a fair price for their cookies and cakes. For a construction worker, the 'economy' is whether general contractors will employ them on a good wage, and for a driving instructor, the 'economy' is whether they have enough young people wanting to learn to drive.

Then, with their earnings, they buy their food and gas, pay their mort-gage or rent, and spend the rest on themselves and their families. Therefore, many people may not know what the Consumer Price Index is, but they sure as hell know what 'inflation' is when they have to pay more for food, gas or rent.

To the question of many Americans perceiving that inflation was too high, I remember Democratic Rep. Katie Porter of California using the line; "Inflation sucks: it's terrible and painful and hard, and I'm committed to fighting it."[20] Fighting it might have included a law against corporate price gouging. Indeed, many price increases were simply greedy companies simply using 'inflation' as an excuse to jack up prices. I recall the CEO of Hershey's in 2022, not even bothering to hide the grift, saying, "Pricing will be an important lever for us this year and is expected to drive most of our growth."[21]

This takes us on to who is better at managing the economy. Despite the Biden Administration's stellar economic record in reducing unemploy-ment, creating jobs, and helping small businesses[22], poll after poll shows voters see the GOP as more competent to handle the economy[23]. This is an age-old problem, yet the explanation is fiendishly straightforward; Republicans are the party of rich people. For receipts, look at how many billionaires came out for Trump in 2024.

We need to employ some critical thinking here. Most Americans are conditioned to believe that rich people became rich and achieved the 'American Dream' by being canny, clever, and competent. Oh, dear reader, if only! The fact is that only 25% of the rich are 'self-made.'

I have a receipt from a bastion of capitalism. In 2022, the Bank of America conducted a study of the wealthy. They reported that 74% of the wealthy inherited their money or were born to rich parents[24]. If you think that is too high, then The Economist and the Roosevelt Institute have also performed studies and come out with about 60% of Americans having been born rich[25].

Sadly, television and the movies have inculcated the Dallas/Kardashian/Trump syndrome of wealthy people being savvy. This cognitive dissonance is given room to breathe because rich people emit an aura of confidence. But, then, so would you if you had millions of dollars in the bank. From that, we confuse their confidence with competence, none of which is helped by our magpie, ratings-addicted friends in the news, who can't stop giddily reporting on the rich and how they have achieved 'The American Dream.'

It was George Carlin who told us, "That's why they call it the American Dream, because you have to be asleep to believe it." George was 100% right. There's no such thing as the English Dream, the Irish Dream, the Swedish Dream, or the Italian Dream. Indeed, nowhere else in the world was this idea sold to people.

Yet, over one hundred and fifty years of conditioning—with a brief intermission between 1945 and 1980 where progressive New Deal policies set in place by President Franklin D. Roosevelt (FDR) allowed for regular folks to lift themselves into the middle class—rich elites have focused Americans on the fact that we can only have nice things when we 'make it.' This would be true if they were talking about Lamborghinis or Learjets. However, what they're actually talking about is education, healthcare, and housing.

From this BS, if you don't 'pull yourself up by your bootstraps,' you're lazy or stupid, and your poverty and desperation are all of your own making. All this conditioning has a further effect of making many regular people very deferential towards the wealthy.

Just look at how the GOP tells voters they need to give tax cuts to the 'makers' to help 'grow' the economy. However, in order to be prudent and maintain a balanced budget, they must also cut spending on 'wasteful' social assistance. Sadly, many low-information voters buy this bunkum. One only needs to look at the $100 billion a year—more than is spent on streaming services and movie and concert tickets combined[26]—Americans spend on lottery tickets. Many of these poor and poorly educated players see luck as the only way out of poverty. And because they aspire to wealth, they may vote for the party that promises not to tax that wealth[27].

Just to return to the American Dream; it's a bizarre paradox that in all those high-income countries where there is no 'Dream,' like England, Sweden, Ireland, and Italy, there is also universal healthcare, pre-K childcare, paid sick leave, paid family leave, and unemployment insurance.

Finally, just to shatter the myth of the GOP being more competent on the economy, I'm bringing some receipts. Between 1945 and 2023, Democrats added over three-quarters of new American jobs. Also, since 1945, ten out of twelve recessions have been under GOP presidents. For just a few examples, Trump gave us one. Bush 43 gave us two, his daddy gave us one, as did Reagan[28].

At this point, allow me to take you on a small detour. It's little commented upon, but since the 1990s, elections have swung like a pendulum. Voters elect Republicans, who promptly slash taxes for their wealthy donors, rack up debt, and crash the economy. The electorate then votes in a Democrat to repair the GOP's economic vandalism. However, come election time, thanks to the far-right's fake culture wars and the corporate media's bothsidesing, the voters forget about the bad times and put a 'strong' and 'decisive' Republican back in office who promptly crashes the economy again. So it is that in 2028, elite Democrats, who live for the status quo, are banking on Trump having crashed the economy and voters sending him packing.

Moving on. Many Americans see the Republicans as stronger on defense, foreign policy, and patriotism. This is simply because Republicans are great at talking tough while wrapping themselves in the flag. They are also extremely quick to use the 'big stick.'

On October 23rd, 1983, a suicide truck bomb was driven into the US Marines barracks in Beirut. It killed 241 service members who had been engaged in a peacekeeping mission in Lebanon[29]. To avenge their deaths and project power, just two days later, Ronald Reagan sent eight thousand troops to the tiny Caribbean island of Grenada, ostensibly to stop a 'domino' from falling under Cuban (Soviet) influence[30].

This smart play saved America from having to send fifty thousand troops to fight an unwinnable war against an invisible enemy in Lebanon. As importantly, Operation Urgent Fury showed the nation its first military victory since WWII and helped both assuage the pain of Lebanon and exorcise the ghosts of Vietnam.

In 1990, former American puppet Saddam Hussein invaded neighboring US ally Kuwait. President George H.W. Bush, to keep our 14 mile per gallon trucks filled with gas, took us to the first Gulf War with Operation Desert Storm. His approval rating hit 88%. Just to note, he only lost the 1992 election because he committed political suicide by raising taxes on regular citizens.

Then in 2001, his son sent troops to Afghanistan to smash the people who thought they could kill America. That was understandable. What was less so was when, in 2003, those same neocons dispatched tens of thousands of troops into an unwinnable war against an invisible enemy in Iraq. Just to note, in 2007, Bush Jr. also crashed the economy, ensuring that the GOP lost the 2008 general election.

Regardless, war—usually after attacks on the US or its interests—has historically been a powerful look for those who start it, offering a "rally round the flag" electoral poll boost. And even when founded upon lies, politicians still get to visit the combat zones and bask in the reflected glory of standing next to heroes.

Conversely, to see the political drag on the party that has to end a war, we just have to look at Lyndon Johnson in Vietnam or Joe Biden in Afghanistan[31].

At this juncture, let's combine both war and weak Democratic messaging. After Russia's invasion of Ukraine in 2022, President Biden provided $68 billion in military aid. This kept the Russian bear at bay. However, with the help of Trump, House speaker Mike Johnson, and the rest of the Confederate Taliban, aid was stalled for six months between October 2023 and April 2024. Cue liberal panic.

What Democrats never bothered telling Americans was that 90% of that $68 billion never left America[32]. It was spent in US factories, making the US artillery shells, US drones, US missiles, and US tanks. This meant well-paid jobs in thirty-one states, many of them red.

At any time during those six months, all Democrats had to do was use the line, "A VOTE AGAINST UKRAINE AID IS A VOTE AGAINST AMERICAN JOBS."

Even Republican voters would have understood that. Then see if Marjorie Taylor Greene or Matt Gaetz dared to vote against it.

Allow me to move us on to 'Law and Order.' Many think this is a GOP strength. This is not surprising, as the right-wing has spent decades increasing funding to, and throwing accolades at, their pals in the police, especially those in the 'inner-cities,' who were cracking skulls and bringing 'order' to 'black chaos.'

As you will read in the chapter 'How to Make Cops Love Liberals,' this was an easy fix for weak Democrats, but they never took it.

I'm not sure what they teach at Democratic Strategist School, but whatever it is, they might want to change the curriculum. 2500 years ago, in ancient Greece, the philosopher Plato wrote, "Rhetoric is the art of ruling the minds of men."[33] Spin forward to today, and Trump, despite his million failings, knows quite a lot about this.

Imagine if he had added fourteen million jobs in just two years, or passed the Infrastructure Act, or been the only president to have visited two active war zones? We would have heard about it morning, noon, and night for five hundred days; no, scratch that, he would have told us ten times a day and had a parade up Washington's Constitution Avenue in his honor.

He is a demented, blundering buffoon, but one of his few true talents, apart from recognizing the basest human instincts in his followers, is his storytelling showmanship and self-promotion. Put more succinctly, it's his hype and bullshit. Allied to that is his ability to lie shamelessly and repeatedly until his lies, whether America being in recession, DEI being the cause of all America's woes, or America being 'invaded' by immigrants—all conveniently parroted by the unquestioning corporate media—get accepted as the 'truth.'

In contrast, most Democratic messaging is like the story at the beginning of the chapter of the meek Dem kid. It's not that they barely report their achievements or bully the media to tell the truth; they actually allow Republicans to steal them and tout them as their own.

To this point, in 2021, the Biden Administration passed the Infrastructure Act, and in 2022, the Inflation Reduction Act. These pieces of legislation represented the very definition of the government working for its citizens. Just to take the IRA. It provided the framework and funds to create hundreds of thousands of jobs, lower health care costs, collect taxes off rich devils, and save your grandkids by promoting clean energy.

The idiotic 'moderate'—and now booted out of office—Democratic Senator for West Virginia, Joe Manchin, ensured it was watered down to just one-third of what it should have been and named it the Inflation Reduction Act. If Dems had just called it what it was, "The Helping Americans Act," people might have been a bit more interested, and Manchin may have had a tougher time neutering it.

Regardless, it meant billions of dollars for workers in industries across America, whether in red or blue states. Yet, in the House, every Republican voted against the IRA. For the Infrastructure Act, 197 out of 210 GOP members voted against it. TRANSLATION: They voted to stop jobs from coming to their districts.

However, when the project money started flowing into their districts, most of those GOP members were exceedingly quick to claim credit for Biden's work[34]. As far as sinisterly smart moves go, I can't admonish Republicans for their naked self-interest. Instead, blame Democrats for never smashing back at them.

This ties into another problem of messaging: so few citizens understand how the billions of dollars of government spending from the Infrastructure and the IRA are actually helping them.

Just to give a couple of examples of how, in the 2024 election, Democrats still had no idea about how to tell stories. Thanks to the IRA, the cost of insulin for seniors on Medicare fell from $275 to $35 a month[35]. That is helping seven million people in red and blue states. It was this simple to message:

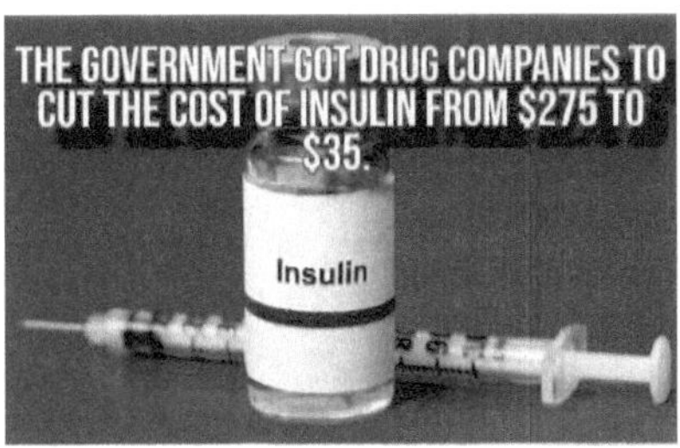

Then, there's asthma. This condition affects twenty-seven million Americans and their families. Inhalers cost up to $489. The IRA smashed the cost down to just $35[36].

As far as those construction projects go, what if every day up to the election, voters had seen billboards, TV, and social media videos of construction projects across America? A bridge in Brooklyn. A road in Raleigh. Water pipes in Wyoming. And the strapline was "YOUR GOVERNMENT TAXES PAID FOR THIS." Do you think they might then think better about 'the government'?

There's more. Every weekday, the White House holds a banal press briefing. During the Biden administration, as far as I could see, it was a sparring match between the press secretary and a tall goon called Peter from the Fox Propaganda network. The only purpose of this spectacle was to provide cheap laughter material for nighttime talk-show hosts.

Why, oh why, wasn't there a huge 160-inch screen behind the press secretary showing a different image or video every day? One day, rural broadband being delivered to Mayes County, Oklahoma. The next, a new bridge coming to Ward County, North Dakota, or new clean water pipes in Flint, Michigan.

Suddenly, these folks would have seen their states and their counties *in Washington,* and they'd feel seen and heard by *Washington*. One should never underestimate how wonderful it is for people to see themselves represented. More importantly, they also would have seen that it was the Democratic-led government that was doing it for them. Then, maybe some of those voters might have voted for the party that was actually helping them.

Chapter 3

How Self-Interest Will Decide If We Live Or Die

Back in 1979, a wise American had these words for the nation,

> We are at a turning point in our history. There are two paths to choose. One is a path I've warned about tonight, the path that leads to fragmentation and self-interest. Down that road lies a mistaken idea of freedom, the right to grasp for ourselves some advantage over others. That path would be one of constant conflict between narrow interests ending in chaos and immobility. It is a certain route to failure.[37]

They were spoken by former President Jimmy Carter and would portend massive wealth inequality, Wall Street's heist of Main Street, and, of course, Trump. But that was the future. The thirty-ninth president was a fine man, undone mainly by the Iranian oil price spike (gasoline comes from oil)[38].

Back then, there was no fracking industry to give us cheap oil, no solar energy, and no wind energy. Thus, to power our big, inefficient cars and trucks, we needed OPEC oil.

Hold that thought. Before we go on, we need to understand that, for everyone, self-interest is their primary motivator. As such, people's lives follow three near immutable truths. They want life to be fair (for them.) They are bad at making decisions. And they don't want an entitlement taken away.

To illustrate the point, let's travel back to 2022. Apart from killing thousands and ruining millions of people's lives, Russia's illegal invasion of Ukraine caused chaos in the world's oil markets. We can think of the resultant (OPEC-influenced) spike in gas prices to over $6 per gallon as Putin's War Tax.

The media and the West are big for Ukraine's fight for freedom against Russian aggression. However, for ordinary people, wherever they live, I'd posit something. Imagine if a new Russian oil company called 'Putin Gas' had opened up, selling gas for $1.50 per gallon. I'd bet everything I own most people would forget about Ukraine and flock to Putin Gas to fill up their pickups and SUVs.

These fuel stations would have queues around the block, not because people are bad, but because it would be in their self-interest. They want life to be fair, and OPEC jacking up the price of oil means that it isn't. But they will have made a bad decision by purchasing Putin Gas that will help an autocrat steal Ukraine from her own people. Notwithstanding that, the entitlement is their ability to continue to drive around in a car or truck that only does 14 miles per gallon.

If that's too micro, just look at the 2024 election. Americans were given the choice between a candidate who promised to help Americans and a candidate who promised to hurt Americans. For millions of voters, their choice was not predicated on whether they or one of the women in their lives may be forced to give birth against her will or whether there would ever be another election. Instead, they claimed to be pissed at having to pay $4.24 for a dozen eggs at Walmart[39].

So, to break it down. They wanted life to be fair—for them—and having to spend more on groceries meant it wasn't. The entitlement was the cheap food that Americans had gotten used to. However, in voting for Trump, these citizens made a bad decision that will doubtless make them much worse off by the time he is (hopefully) voted out of office in 2028.

Now that we have four more years of Trump, something else that will get much worse is global warming. Today, emissions from internal combustion engine (ICE) cars and trucks account for one-fifth of all global warming[40]. Among liberals and academics, a narrative exists that, in order to prevent catastrophe, we have to make sacrifices, like driving our cars less or turning down the heat in our houses[41]—things that make our lives worse.

For many people, the problem of global warming is too big and too scary to think about. This takes us to those liberal politicians who don't understand that voters need to feel hope that the future will be better than the past. Fortunately, solutions exist today to save us humans while at the same time benefiting us.

I despise the oil-producing, planet-heating Saudi and Russian governments. This being said, for a long time, even though I had the means, I wasn't willing to sell my ICE car to help solve the problem. Obviously, that makes me a hypocrite. However, recently, I bought a Nissan Leaf electric vehicle (EV). My principal reason for purchase was not because I am crying about pollution or global warming. I bought an EV because my home electricity supplier offers cheap electricity.

On this note, I checked electricity costs in Texas. They are as low as $0.11 per kilowatt-hour (kWh)[42]. The 40 kWh battery in my car takes me 140 miles, which means it would only cost me about $4 to drive 140 miles. This is the figure that blows people away, as it's three times what a Toyota Prius hybrid can get. If we want to have any hope of solving global warming, just cut the crap and start telling people an EV can travel "140 MILES ON JUST $4." Then, they know it's going to save them money.

I might not have convinced some of you yet. I know the fear stories about EV batteries catching fire or EVs breaking down and costing tens of thousands of dollars to fix. It's all BS, but it's great for corporate media and social media clicks.

Here's the real story. An EV only has about thirty low-stressed parts in the powertrain, as opposed to the 3,000 parts in an ICE car. This means much cheaper maintenance costs, as there is much less to go wrong. Indeed, an EV will easily have a lifespan of at least two or three times that of an ICE car. My receipts? Today, there are Teslas, under ten years old, that have covered over 400,000 miles, still running on the original battery and motors[43].

To entice people to buy EVs, the Biden administration offered new car buyers $7500 rebates. If only they had split that between new EVs and used EVs (what ordinary Americans buy.) Also, it could have mandated for every manufacturer who wanted to sell in the US car market—whether Ford,

Tesla, or Toyota—that their batteries must be warranted for 10 years or 250,000 miles, whichever comes sooner.

Now, apart from getting cheaper cars, owners would be confident any problem would be covered under the manufacturer's warranty. Suddenly, the used car market in EVs would take off, which means more new EVs can be sold. That's great news for American auto workers and manufacturers, and it wouldn't have cost Uncle Sam or the consumer one cent.

There's more. In later chapters, you will read about generating $0.10 a kWh local electricity from local solar and wind by making friends with farmers to use some of the farmland that makes up nearly half of America.

To the point of NIMBYs (Not In My Back Yards) complaining about solar and wind spoiling their view, watch how quickly they quiet down when they are the ones taking advantage of the $0.10 per kWh electricity and the jobs that come from making it.

You'll note I haven't said one word about reducing carbon emissions, parts per million, or Net Zero, because as long as folks know that the future will be better and cheaper, it will be in their self-interest to want it.

As you read on, you will see how self-interest will be a motivator for winning over urban folks, rural folks, and even cops. In fact, self interest will be the reason that Democrats could secure a landslide in 2028.

Chapter 4

The Government Life-Support Machine Which Ensures That Ayn Rand's Disciples Never Go Bankrupt.

In 1980, Ronald Reagan offered a perfect distillation of Ayn Rand's (we will come to her later) selfish musings that have infected every corner of Republican and conservative thinking today;

> I've always felt the nine most terrifying words in the English language are: I'm from the Government, and I'm here to help[44].

A counterweight to this came from Senator Elizabeth Warren, speaking in 2011 about what the government actually does;

> There is nobody in this country who got rich on his own — nobody. You moved your goods to market on the roads the rest of us paid for. You hired workers the rest of us paid to educate. You were safe in your factory because of police-forces and fire-forces that the rest of us paid for.[45]

Conservative thinkers of the old school Reagan/Bush era aspire to low spending, low regulation, low taxes, and strong national defense; in other words, 'small government.' However, there's something about their thinking I could never square. After all, it's the government that provides Americans with healthcare, social security, education, defense, and all the infrastructure spending on bridges, roads, and tunnels. Also, it's the government who tries to make sure that Exxon Mobil doesn't murder the planet, Boeing's planes don't fall out of the sky, and Mad Musk's self-driving Teslas don't mow down school children. It's also the government that ensures that if a bank gambles away your family's money, you get compensation.

The point I will make in this chapter is not just how government helps, but that 'the government' is *you*, whether you are a nurse in New Jersey, a delivery driver in Delaware, or a salesman in South Carolina. You, the taxpayer, are paying for government, and you may be quite surprised at what, and indeed, who, you are paying for.

A perfect illustration of government working was during the coronavirus pandemic in 2020. Pharmaceutical companies did absolutely nothing to produce a vaccine right until the point that the government guaranteed to buy every dose of vaccine they produced.

Then, suddenly, the factory lights were switched on, the machines roared into action, and the race got underway to produce a workable vaccine. Pfizer and Moderna won through, and, as of 2023, they had sold 1.2 billion doses, earning their stockholders a risk-free government (taxpayer)-guaranteed $25 billion[46].

Without the government, they would have ambled along, concerned only about ripping off Medicare and American consumers, all to increase their profits, allowing them to buy back their stock to boost the stock price, to which the CEO's and boards' pay and compensation packages are linked[47].

This puts me in mind of the phrase 'corporate socialism[48].' It's this that allows mega-corps to survive on juicy multi-billion-dollar government contracts and for Wall Street to be pumped full of financial cocaine, a.k.a stimulus.

Which segues us to the world's richest troll, Mad Musk. The owner of Tesla and Twitter is neither a creator nor an inventor nor a scientist. By pure luck, his takeover of the already-existing Tesla electric car company coincided with the transition to electric cars and zero emissions. While I will never deny the brilliance of his diverse pool of workers, what few people may know is that just fifteen years ago, Tesla was on the verge of bankruptcy.

Just for clarification, today, Musk rails against the 'government'; all while he pockets massive government subsidies for both Tesla and his SpaceX rocket company[49].

However, back in 2009, his plans for expansion coincided with the moment that the bankers imploded the world. Musk needed urgent cash to buy his first factory at the former GM-Toyota site in Fremont, California, and he was a hair's breadth away from being just another crazy dreamer with a big idea that didn't go anywhere.

But then he got lucky, and the Obama Administration's Department of Energy, a.k.a. "THE FEDERAL GOVERNMENT," came to his rescue, giving him a $500 million no-strings-attached loan to get him out of his hole[50]. Without that, there would be no Tesla, no SpaceX, no Starlink, no Twitter, and no Musk.

To echo Elizabeth Warren's words from the opening of the chapter, one of the main reasons (apart from the two-thirds who were born rich) that these oligarchs can get rich is because they are doing business in the most advanced society on earth, paid for and built off the backs of you and your hardworking parents and grandparents.

It's government subsidies (your taxes) that help build Musk's factories. His workers are educated in government schools. It's the government (your taxes) that funds research into the new technologies that Tesla uses, and the government that pays for the courts that guarantee their patents are not infringed. It's the government (your taxes) that funds the highways that Tesla's car transporters travel down, and it's the government (your taxes) that negotiates the favorable trade agreements that allow Tesla to trade overseas. Oh, and it's government subsidies (your taxes) that give Tesla billions of dollars of environmental credits[51] and also the $7500 federal discount to customers for purchasing a Tesla[52].

You don't have to believe me about how much the rich and corporations have benefited from the government-funded infrastructure. Here's a receipt from Amazon founder Jeff Bezos speaking in 2023;

> When I started Amazon, I didn't have to develop a payment system. It already existed. It was called the credit card. I didn't have to develop a transportation system to deliver the packages. It already existed. It was called the Postal Service and Royal Mail and Deutsche Post and so on. So all this heavy lifting infrastructure was already in place, and I could stand on its shoulders[53].

Something else the government does is fund the military. I'm sure many people are puzzled where all the $916 billion (2023) the government spends on the military goes[54] . Well, to companies like Boeing, General Dynamics, Lockheed Martin, and Raytheon. These are the corporations that build the Abrams tanks, F-35 fighters, Predator drones, and Tomahawk missiles. Their factories are spread over all fifty states.

This means—aside from massive profits for those corporations—jobs for almost every congressional district, and as jobs mean votes, who's going to turn a job away? Back in 1961, President Dwight Eisenhower warned us of the "military-industrial complex"[55]: defense contractors enriching themselves and their stockholders by milking the taxpayer[56]. But also, today, that $1,000,000,000,000 complex is a massive American job creation program; both are effectively beautiful acts of government "socialism."

If you will allow me a slight segue into weak Democratic messaging. Few people know, but nearly a third of the federal government workforce of 2.2 million employees are veterans[57]. Yet, Democrats never bothered to tell you that one in three government workers are veterans and that they love helping veterans get meaningful employment after their service. Many of these former service personnel are disabled, and it was the 1944 Veterans Preference Act that allowed the government, through DEI, to ensure that wounded veterans were never forgotten, and to employ their skills to help the land they helped defend[58]. This is what "thank you for your service" means in action.

Going back to the pharmaceutical companies. We know about the COVID vaccines, but these clever characters couldn't get to be as powerful as they are today without helping to pass the Bayh-Dole Act back in 1979[59]. Up to that time, the government and taxpayers owned the drug patents. This ensured that for your parents or grandparents, drug prices were low. Those low prices for consumers also meant low but steady profits for drug companies.

Alas, the Ayn Rand brigade didn't like this, and the Bayh-Dole Act ensured that from 1980 onwards, they owned all the patents. So it is that now they can luxuriate in the profits from twenty-year patents on drugs discovered in government-funded hospitals and research laboratories, all paid for by your taxes[60].

Despite this, today, drug companies fight tooth and claw to ensure that taxpayers who paid for the research that discovered the drugs keep on paying extortionate prices for those drugs[61]. Sometimes, up to 10x what a citizen in Britain, Canada, or France would pay.

Democrats have been working to redress these issues. However, as the largest lobbyists in Washington, drug companies spend over $378 million a year bribing mostly GOP politicians to keep prices high[62]. It works. For a receipt, every GOP rep voted against the Inflation Reduction Act.

It was only thanks to Democrats that the IRA passed and forced drug companies to lower the prices of ten widely used drugs, including insulin and asthma inhalers[63]. However, dear reader, don't think Big Pharma went quietly into the night. Even today, they are spending tens of millions of dollars in litigation to keep Americans paying high prices[64]. Doubtless, after the 2024 election, they will have a free pass to jack prices back up.

Nonetheless, for any conservatives still reading who think that before the wonderful pharma companies came to our rescue, Americans must have been dropping like flies, not quite. Smallpox was eliminated by 1949, rubella in 1964, mumps in 1967, and polio in 1979[65].

Then throw into the mix the conundrum that back then, the top rate of income tax was over 70% and corporation taxes were over 50%, and it's no surprise the powerful want to gaslight people into hating 'taxes' and 'the government.'

As to trying to understand the mindset of many of the elites that we have read about so far, we need to meet Ayn Rand. When you grasp her "objectivism" ideas, you'll have an eureka moment. Literally, everything that's happened economically since Reagan in 1980 is Ayn Rand 1.01.

Rand lived with her parents in Russia at the time of the 1917 Communist revolution. The parents owned a pharmacy that the Communists took from them without compensation. The family fled to America. Unsurprisingly, Ayn was fiercely anti-Communist and wanted the world to know it. However, she wasn't smart enough to challenge existing orthodoxies in philosophy, but she enjoyed writing and could combine her ideas into her stories.

So it would be she wrote two books that rocked the mid-twentieth-century conservative establishment: The Fountainhead in 1943 and Atlas Shrugged in 1957. Within the 752 pages of seductive, simple stupidity that is The Fountainhead, we meet Howard Roark. He's an architect going against the grain of the traditional establishment by wanting to construct Modernist buildings.

So far, so little man-up-against-the-system. But here's the problem. Howard Roark doesn't believe in rules and doesn't believe in regulations. He only believes in himself and will stop at nothing and trample over anyone to get where he wants.

Moving on to 1947's Atlas Shrugged, over nearly 1200 pages, readers are treated to the vision of John Galt. This charismatic engineer is furious at the 'socialist world' of regulation and taxation ('looting'), and along with some other wealthy devils ('Men of Minds') goes on a rich people's strike by moving to Galt's Gulch in the Colorado mountains. Here, these unshackled sociopathic narcissists seek to wait out societal collapse—inevitable in their minds absent their unsurpassed magnificence—in order to remake America in their own selfish hyper-capitalist image.

These books were the dog-eat-dog and the scarcity mindset writ large. Rand called her 'philosophy', "Objectivism". She also wrote a series of essays entitled, with no sense of irony, "The Virtue of Selfishness."[66] This was catnip for the conservative set, who'd been looking for a justification to get the government out of the way so they could plunder.

At this point, you probably want a receipt;

> Not only was I a strong supporter of Ayn Rand. I wouldn't change anything. I still think she was right, and I have learned a great deal from her.[67]

That was former Federal Reserve Chair Alan Greenspan speaking to Vanity Fair in the year 2000. He was in charge of the Fed between 1987 and 2006, just about the time that his Randian policies, combined with Bill Clinton's financial deregulation, were fueling the unregulated financial fires that would melt down the world's economic system in 2007.

In 2008, with Wall Street bailed out but Main Street bankrupted, 82-year-old Greenspan offered this mea culpa;

> I discovered a flaw in the model that I perceived is the critical functioning structure that defines how the world works. I had been going for 40 years with considerable evidence that it was working exceptionally well.[68]

To meet Rand's heartiest devotees is to enter a crow's nest of con men and cruel men. Despite it stretching the bounds of credulity that he could have read a 752-page book, Trump claims to love Rand[69]. Mad Musk is also a fan[70]. So are most of the Silicon Valley robber barons who ushered in the era of 'move fast and break things'[71].

Obviously, as selfishness is a guiding principle of the GOP, they adore Rand[72]. Despite her being fiercely anti-religious, a somewhat bastardized version of her ideas lives within Project 2025. This would slash government spending on social programs to pave the way for massive cuts for the wealthy. After all, reprehensible Randians are rich enough that they can afford to pay for private schools for their kids, and private healthcare for them and their families, so they don't see why they should have to pay for your family's education and healthcare.

What remained of government spending would fund the military, Homeland Security, the police, and the courts. To understand why. Republicans need the military to continue modern manifest destiny by securing existing and seeking new markets for American corporations to sell Barbies, Boeings, and Big Macs. The courts will be there to ensure that the law always favors them and their oligarchs, while criminalizing dissent, and the police (and maybe some Homeland Security and military too) will be required to keep the millions of angry, discontented Americans in line.

Returning to the story of Ayn Rand, we must head to a familiar town called Hypocrisy. It is here that we find a perfect summation of her and her selfish anti-government philosophy. After contracting lung cancer from years of heavy cigarette smoking, she had few qualms about grabbing government Medicare for her treatment. As if that cheek wasn't enough, no moral or philosophical impediments restrained this champion of conservative values from cashing her monthly government social security check[73].

Chapter 5

American Hostile Takeover: The People Who Are Really Stealing Your Country

If Trump really meant 'MAKE AMERICA GREAT AGAIN,' rather than 'MAKE AMERICA WHITE AGAIN,' he would have explained to his supporters how a good-paying union job meant a good life. Obviously, he didn't, but if any of you have MAGA relations, then perhaps these words will resonate with them;

Do you recall a time when the income of a single school-teacher or baker or salesman or mechanic was enough to buy a home, have two cars, and raise a family? I do. In the 1950s, my father, Ed Reich, had a shop on the main street of a nearby town, in which he sold women's clothing to the wives of factory workers. He earned enough for the rest of us to live comfortably. We weren't rich but never felt poor, and our standard of living rose steadily through the 1950s and 1960s. That used to be the norm. For three decades after World War II, America created the largest middle class the world had ever seen. During those years the earnings of the typical American worker doubled, just as the size of the American economy doubled. Over the last thirty years, by contrast, the size of the economy doubled again but the earnings of the typical American went nowhere.[74]

That was the brilliantly insightful former secretary of state for labor, Robert Reich, writing in his 2015 book, 'Saving Capitalism,' about what your parents and grandparents may have experienced of the 'American Dream.'[75]

That notion took off in 1933 with Franklin Roosevelt's New Deal of great social programs and trade union protections. From those foundations, through hard work and a little luck, an American could buy themselves a nice house and build a decent life. The 'dream' more or less died under Ronald Reagan, and today many Americans, especially young people, don't think the economy is working for them. They are correct.

Capitalism only needed to keep two promises. First, it had to put bread and milk on the shelves at affordable prices. Then, there was the expectation that every generation would be better off than the previous one.

After World War Two, to help this along, there were the suburbs. These started in 1947 with the Levittowns, 17,000 mass-manufactured houses, first built in Long Island, New York, and then in Pennsylvania and New Jersey. They were around one thousand square feet plus an attic, all with TV, and HI Fi, and just a 5% down payment was required, or 0% if you were a veteran. If your grandparents bought a house in Levittown in 1950 for $7,990, they would have seen it rise in value to $389,900 today[76].

The safety and security of that home in the suburbs gave them the opportunity to give their children a low-stress upbringing. This helped those children have the best chance of attaining a good life and buying their own home. Indeed, homeownership is the very definition of being middle-class.

However, it never would have happened without the federal government subsidizing the home loans. Thank the Democratic Truman administration for that. They realized both the power of helping to create middle-class homeownership and of creating middle-class jobs in its construction. Of course, then, it was only for white folks.

That being said, today, for 90% of people, the home they are diligently paying off the mortgage on will be their nest egg and their biggest asset. I would argue that a good part of the fury in modern America, especially from men, isn't any of the fake culture issues like LGBTQ+, 'woke,' immigration, or women's rights. Mostly, it's the inability of people to have one job that pays enough to allow them to buy an affordable house that will become their home and a place to realize dreams, make memories, and, one day, pass on to their children.

To that point. I was one of the lucky people to be born as a Gen X man. When I grew up, there were no wars to fight, no financial depression, no social media, jobs were plentiful, and houses cost less than 4x earnings.

Back in 1992, without an expensive college degree, I got a job in the City of London at Shearson Lehman Hutton, the same bank that would become *the* Lehman Brothers, who helped to crash the world economy in 2008. I worked as a junior analyst in the Mergers and Acquisitions Department. I'd like you to bear with me whilst I show you how this world works. I promise it will be worth the read.

Ours, like every other bank, had what was called a 'Chinese Wall.' That is an imaginary wall to stop us from sharing inside information with our traders or salesmen. The reason for that 'wall' was that we were acting for corporate clients whose companies would merge or be acquired.

It was like having a crystal ball. Because we had this 'inside information,' we knew what the future stock price would be. This was perfectly legal, right up to where someone broke the 'Chinese Wall' and either shared it with the traders or salesmen or gave it to someone else, who could then make the best type of bet, the *unlosable* one.

To drive this point home, I feel I must enlist the help of a Wall Street titan;

> Greed is all right, by the way,". "I want you to know that. I think greed is healthy. You can be greedy and still feel good about yourself.[77]

That was Ivan Boesky, channeling Ayn Rand, speaking to graduates at the University of California in 1986. Boesky was a man with a messiah-like talent for picking the exact right time to buy and sell stocks.

However, it transpired that his 'magic touch' was less Midas and more paying off minions in investment banks and brokerage firms to give him inside information. For his troubles, he would serve two years in prison and pay a $100 million fine. Still, as a consolation, his infamy was the inspiration for Michael Douglas's character, Gordon Gekko, in Oliver Stone's 1987 movie, Wall Street.

As Boesky went down, he took with him another Whale of Wall Street, Michael Milken of Drexel Burnham Lambert. Known as the Junk Bond King, this character pioneered the financial alchemy of turning worthless debt into an asset. Milken was another gentleman with a suspiciously sterling track record of never losing—because he too was cheating!![78]

This is how many wealthy people just keep making money. They have contacts, who are lawyers, bankers, or accountants, who will share the 'inside information' to allow for the unlosable bet. Fortunately for the rich, insider trading is nearly impossible to detect or prove, and besides, next to no one is interested in prosecuting rich people.

It's a basic truth that it's so much easier to arrest Jamal from New York's South Bronx for holding a few grams of marijuana than it is to build a watertight case against Jeffrey, the banker from the Upper East Side. Jamal can't put up a fight, and anyway, his public defender has far too many other cases. Jeffrey, however, probably has enough juice to get someone at City Hall to drop the charges long before he'd ever see the inside of a courtroom.

Knowing that may illustrate why it's so hard to pass a ban on members of Congress trading in stocks. The fact that half the members of Congress are millionaires doesn't help[79]. In this book, you will see how hypocrisy is not a disease that liberals are immune from.

To this point, we can speak about the 'Nancy Pelosi Stock Tracker' app that tracks the former speaker's stock market trades, executed by her husband, Paul. This gentleman also had a Midas-like touch where stocks were concerned. Indeed, in 2023, Mr. Pelosi's trades increased in value by 45%[80].

In fighting against the stock trading ban that any fifth grader would understand was necessary, meritocratic Nancy offered this defense of congressional stock trading: "We are a free-market economy. They should be able to participate in that."[81]

Today, Nancy and Paul are worth a not inconsiderable $114 million[82]. They, alongside others with over $11 million in assets, make up the richest

1% of Americans. According to the Federal Reserve, the total wealth of that richest 1% amounts to $43 trillion. Most of the increase has taken place since 1980[83].

The economist David Ricardo coined the idea of "rent seeking" nearly three hundred years ago[84]. By design, rent-seeking is opaque and complicated. However, you may have heard politicians, like Bernie Sanders, speak of the 'rigged system.' In part, he is alluding to rent- seeking.

It can be where businesses seek tariffs on competitors or rig the law to allow for monopoly power in their business, but it also applies to any case of the rich engineering situations to profit themselves.

These could be tech companies that fight regulations that would keep us safe but hurt their profits. Or drug companies that fight regulations that would lower their prices but hurt their profits. Or Wall Street banks, who make themselves too big to fail but demand our bailouts when they nearly do.

Invariably, rent-seeking makes ordinary people's lives more expensive. Effectively, the rich are our landlords, and we are forced to 'rent' America from them. And the more rent that we pay them, the more influence they can buy, and the more influence they can buy, the more powerful they get.

By way of illustration, let me take you into the world of private equity. They used to be called corporate raiders, and before that, asset strippers. Whatever title we use, this 'industry' is worth $7.2 trillion, or one quarter of the whole US economy[85]. Allow me a few paragraphs to show you how these rent-seeking demons can crash into ordinary folks' lives.

To understand their business model, we can look at an imaginary company called 'Private Equity Inc.' 'P.E. Inc's' purpose is to find asset-rich businesses and, using borrowed money (debt), pay too much for them (but don't worry, they have a plan).

Let's imagine that P.E. Inc. has borrowed $100 million to buy a residential care home business called 'We Care Inc.,' which has two hundred and fifty well-run care homes across America. Just to note, the care home industry is completely dependent on government funding (through Medicaid) to pay the $116,000 annual costs for each resident[86]. Notwithstanding that, caring is a cost-intensive business that no one used to get into in order to get rich. So you may wonder how the new owners survive when they have debt interest payments as high as 19% to make. Here's where the 'magic' happens.

P. E. Inc. start by splitting We Care Inc into an operating company and a property company. The two hundred and fifty care homes, each one worth $5 million, into a separate property company called 'We Care. Inc (Property.)' They sell the homes, with the new owners leasing them back to We Care Inc (Operating).

Through their 'canny business skills,' P.E. Property Inc. has earned $125 million dollars from selling off the family silver. We Care Inc. (Operating) has not only lost its properties (assets) without receiving any cash, but now also has the burden of renting something that it once owned.

The private equity business model has a '2 and 20' fee structure[87]. They charge We Care Inc. (Operating) a 2% annual management fee and receive 20% from any profits they make, but as they are separate from We Care Inc. (Operating), they are not liable for any of the firm's losses. Thus, from selling off the properties, they can pay off the original $100 million business loan and make We Care Inc. (Operating) pay them their $25 million fees out of the 'profits' it made from 'selling' off their homes.

This is what sinister financial alchemy looks like. The private equity ghouls have taken a decent, well-run company with solid assets and sold off those assets. Then they have stripped out all that money and left nothing in its place. Now you see why they used to be called "asset strippers" and today are known as 'vultures capitalists'.[88]

Here's where things get even more tricky for We Care Inc. (Operating). It needs to keep making a profit to pay its staff and its costs. However, the company has no assets, so no collateral for any loans, yet they still have to make rental payments on 250 care homes. So, all they can do is slash costs.

Thus, instead of a caring staffing ratio of one member of staff for every seven patients, they cut it down to one to fourteen[89]. Then, rather than healthy, homemade meals for your vulnerable relatives, they buy frozen 'mystery-meat' dinners. But it's never enough, as the debt keeps demanding to be paid. So they sell the care home minibus that was used to take the residents out into the world.

Now, without being able to look forward to exciting adventures, all the residents have to occupy themselves with are four walls, a TV, and a mouthful of sedatives.

Even with all these stormy waters buffeting We Care Inc. (Operating), the company can still just about stay in business because, in America, there are more patients than care homes, and Medicaid pays for over two-thirds of care home residents[90]. The problem is that to make up the money to meet the debt payments, the managers must take in more high-needs and high-care patients, such as those with serious Alzheimer's or dementia; Medicaid will pay twice as much for their care[91].

So now, the caring, hardworking staff of We Care Inc. (Operating) are still working for the same pay, but with twice the number of patients, many of whom have extremely demanding conditions[92].

I wonder if they know it's the sweat of their labor paying for their private equity bosses' Gulfstream jet? Perhaps the same jet that's sent to pick up Justice Clarence Thomas and whisk him off on a $500,000 holiday, just before he votes on a case involving the regulation of staffing levels in care homes?

It should hardly surprise you that, given how avaricious this business model is, in up to 40% of private equity cases, the businesses they take over go bust, and their workers are made redundant. But the private equity bosses aren't concerned, as they've earned their profits and paid back the Wall Street loans, so their credit is good. Now, they can just start again with another business.

Most people will never know about this toxic yet perfectly legal business model, because the only people who lose out are the employees and, in this case, the residents. It's just another example of the Mistresses of Wall Street screwing the people on Main Street.

Should you think I'm some insane fool, I will let a man with unimpeachable conservative credentials offer you his take on it;

> If someone who is very wealthy comes in and takes over your company and takes out all the cash and leaves behind the unemployment. I think that's not a model we want to advocate, and I don't think any conservative wants to get caught defending that kind of model[93].

That was far-right GOP firebrand Newt Gingrich speaking to Fox News back in 2012. Ostensibly, he was speaking against the private equity billionaire and presidential candidate, Mitt Romney. Of course, that was then. Today, this vapid viper would probably breakdance on a burger bun for a few private equity dollars.

Sadly, this vulture capitalism model works especially well for any captive market business. Indeed, anywhere these fiends can jack up customer costs to reward themselves and/or leech off the taxpayer, you will find them. They own hospitals—where they can charge $7 for a Band-Aid[94] and $91 for a bag of saline (salt water)[95]—water companies, electricity companies, veterinary practices, and even housing[96].

For the latter, they can buy up thousands of properties, paying much more than a regular American can, because they have a plan. Once they own the houses (assets), citizens have no choice but to rent them. Housing is a dream business for these devils, as it offers both the rising asset price of the home and the ability to put up the rents in order to pay off their loans[97].

Private equity cannot operate without loans from Wall Street banks. This leads us on to why I use the term 'Mistresses of Wall Street.' In the 1980s, about the time of Ivan Boesky, author Tom Wolfe satirically called them "Masters of the Universe."[98] However, this affords them a status far exceeding their value. Instead, I call them 'Mistresses', for they look great in their $2000 suits, cost a fortune in maintenance (bailouts and stimulus), and never stop screwing us.

These Wall Street characters came of age in the 1980s with the BS Ayn Rand lies that cutting taxes for rich people meant that some of their wealth would, like a champagne tower, "trickle down."

It's no coincidence that this mindset coincided with the largest ever federal and trade deficits. Also, these 'Mistresses' have, since 1980, visited upon us three financial crashes and dozens of frauds, including Enron, WorldCom, Madoff, and the current crypto con[99].

The Mistresses have only three solid 'talents': speculating, obtaining rent from the Federal Reserve (stimulus), and cooking up new ways to defraud hardworking Americans out of their savings. On that note, Gordon Gecko's "greed is good" mentality seemed almost quaint when compared to what the morons did in 2008.

This is not the forum to re-document the financial crisis. Just note, it could never have happened without Bill Clinton, who threw away the Glass-Steagall Act regulations that separated retail banking from investment banking in 1999. It was that which allowed your steady deposit-taker to suddenly go full Las Vegas and gamble all your money away[100].

Outside of the Mistresses of Wall Street, Silicon Valley, and the pharmaceutical companies, there are other rent seekers who have your worst interests at heart. A 2019 study, "Capitalists in the Twenty-First Century,"[101] shed light on some of the 140,000 Americans who earn over $1.58 million per year, putting them well within the richest 1%.

These are the people who most directly impact ordinary Americans' lives, and many are here to make sure that life will be as expensive as they can make it.

They are the owners of auto dealerships, auto repair shops, gas stations, beverage distributors, business equipment contractors, and fast-food franchises. Their wealth comes from the fact that they own the business and aren't reliant on salary, but it's also about what kind of business they own.

Remember what you read earlier about 'rent seeking.' So it is that many of these businesses are the protected ones. This is from the New York Times,

> Auto dealerships have legal protections; state franchising laws often give auto dealers exclusive rights to sell cars in a territory. Same for many beverage distributors, which act as middlemen between alcohol companies and stores and supermarkets. Beverage distributors have long been protected by a system set up after Prohibition that prevents beverage companies from distributing their products themselves.[102]

On the matter of auto dealerships. Very few people know how huge a business it is. The National Automobile Dealers Association (NADA) represents 16,773 franchised light-vehicle dealers[103]. In 2022, they sold 13.7 million light-duty vehicles at a value of $1.2 trillion[104]. Put into perspective, it's the sixth-largest business in America, bigger than life insurance and just below commercial banking. If franchised auto dealers were a country, they would have a larger economy than Saudi Arabia[105].

None of this happened by accident. NADA is a powerful lobbyist. It donates more than the NRA to the Republican party at local, state, and national levels. What they lobby against are the things that would save you money and make you safer, like better fuel standards or crash protection regulations. This is useful when 14 mpg, three-ton light-duty passenger trucks are their members' most profitable products.

The rigged system doesn't just happen in the automotive sector. Historian Patrick Wyman wrote about the concentration of wealth in his former hometown of Yakima in Washington State. Despite only having a population of just under 100,000 people, it's a story that echoes much of America's.

> Commercial agriculture is a lucrative industry, at least for those who own the orchards, the cold-storage units, the processing facilities, and the large businesses that cater to them...The owners are mostly white; the laborers are mostly Latino, a significant portion of them undocumented immigrants who often work under brutally difficult circumstances. Ownership of the real, core assets is where the region's wealth comes from, and it doesn't extend down the social hierarchy.[106]

We are going to have an honest conversation about the southern border, 'illegal immigration,' and those rich bosses in chapter eleven. For now, apart from agriculture, we can look at construction and meat processing. These are also rent-seeking industries with a record of using undocumented labor and fighting against unions and safety legislation.

One connecting factor of these businesses is that their owners form a whole chunk of the 'rich' part of the SCARI coalition of GOP voters. For them, regulation and state taxes are a bind. Which takes us to the heart of the issue; it's always about profit.

Knowing all this should have made it easy for Democrats to position themselves as the party for the people who receive the paycheck rather than the people who write the paycheck. But here's where things get a little complicated and also explains, partly, why they lost in 2024. The 'meritocracy' is the notion that we deserve everything we get, even if two-thirds of the rich were born into it or inherited it.

It's an affliction that taints liberals and conservatives alike. In his milestone 2017 book "Listen, Liberal", Thomas Frank wrote of an inflection point for the Democratic Party way back in 1971. That was the point they decided to pivot away from the working class towards the college-educated class.

Mr. Frank describes "The Coalition of the Ascendant," that included many professionals. That word 'professional' is important, as you can't be a professional—a doctor, banker, journalist or lawyer—without a college degree and, in many cases, a postgraduate degree. It's no coincidence these "credentialed" jobs are the best paying and also those that society looks upon as the most prestigious.

At this point, I feel an anecdote may be useful. I recall asking my—now 25-year-old—godchildren, when they were at school, whether they had done their homework. Their answer was priceless: "We're not interested in that Shakespeare shit."

That they have mild dyslexia didn't help with academic life. But there's a deeper truth. My godchildren, like many kids, really weren't interested in ancient Rome, Shakespeare, or Venn diagrams. It doesn't mean that they are stupid or lazy. It's just how people are.

School failed them by not recognizing that they were 'hands' people rather than 'pen' people. This is a peril of standardized testing.

Society might also have failed them. It was only by chance that their father knew a local businessman who gave them the benefit of the doubt. So it is today they can operate the twenty-ton road planing machine that repairs your highway. They can also fix a broken excavator in the middle of a muddy field and build a barn from scratch.

Now answer this. Who do you think is more useful to the world, an investment banker, a management consultant, or my godchildren?

Yet, because the meritocratic system favors the professional class, it doesn't include technical colleges for the two-thirds of working Americans without a college degree. Thus, perversely, it excludes people—who may not be as fortunate as my godchildren—but who can also build rather than create.

The meritocratic mindset also explains why liberals, except for Joe Biden, Bernie Sanders, Alexandria Ocasio-Cortez, Jasmine Crockett, Tim Walz, and a sprinkling of others, don't talk about unions or stand alongside fighters like United Auto Workers President Shawn Fain. It's also why we don't see harsh anti-union laws like "right to work" challenged.

Elite Democratic voters and donors see unions as standing against their belief that the individual, of whatever background, gender, class, or color, can rise, as far and as fast as their talents allow.

You may see a disconnect there. After all, those same unions operate as a collective to press for good wages, medical care, and sick pay for many non-college-educated workers.

The meritocratic mindset also allows many liberals to ignore inequality, whether in housing, taxation, or earnings. For them, if you want a good house, then go to college and get qualified, and if you want to earn more money, go to college and get qualified, and if you don't, then why are you surprised that you're poor?

It didn't work out too well in the 2024 election. Part of the reason for Trump's victory was the collapse in the Gen Z vote for Democrats. Some of this was apathy, but in polling, abortion fell behind the economy, and in particular, young people's inability to get on the housing ladder[107]. Bear in mind, the median price of a single-family home in 2024 is $400,000, and you may understand their frustrations.

One way to win back some of these disaffected Americans would be a massive nationwide house-building program. In chapter ten, you will see how inner cities could be rebuilt by bringing in young people. As far as the suburbs and exurbs go, I'm thinking of the Homestead Act crossed with tiny Levittowns. Using rezoned agricultural or federal land (the government owns nearly one-third of America's 2.2 billion acres), developers could build tracts of one-hundred-home developments[108].

As a step in the right direction, the 2024 Harris campaign offered (quietly) to guarantee the down payment for new home buyers[109]. Now imagine if families could get hold of a 1300-square-foot modern modular factory-built home for around $250,000[110]. And remember, these homes would be made in America, using American labor and materials. Which means millions upon millions of new jobs. Do you imagine that might be an election-winning policy?

Chapter 6

Corporate Media: The 'Referee' Who Always Sides With MAGA.

"It May Not Be Good for America, but It's Damn Good for CBS." These were the hideously honest and supremely cynical words of Leslie Moonves, the CEO of CBS, following Trump's 2016 election. You may think he was just an outlier, a greedy, gluttonous gargoyle standing adrift from the Sentinels of Freedom guarding the gates of democracy.

Well, not quite. To set straight the nonsense of the 'liberal media,' in 2020, the weird and ghoulish billionaire boss of Politico, Mathias Döpfner, was reported to have told his staff to *pray* for a Trump victory[111]. And another toxic right-wing billionaire, John Malone, who was big on Trump, controlled CNN up to 2023 and heavily pushed the old both-sides argument[112].

This is all a long way from the age of Walter Cronkite. Known as 'the most trusted man in America,' he was the anchorman for the CBS evening news between 1962 and 1981[113]. Cronkite was the staple who brought into American homes some of the most consequential events of the mid-20th century: the JFK assassination, civil rights, the moon landings, and the Vietnam War. Cronkite was quoted as saying;

I think it is absolutely essential in a democracy to have competition in the media, a lot of competition, and we seem to be moving away from that.[114]

We didn't listen, and so, today, when you hear the words "corporate media," it is because just five corporations own 90% of all broadcast TV media in the US. Just for context, in 1983, it was fifty[115]. These five corporations, Comcast (NBC), News Corp (Fox), Viacom (CBS), AT&T (CNN), and Disney (ABC), need to sell advertising to make profits to ensure that Wall Street analysts leave their stock as a BUY and never as a SELL.

Later on, we will talk about the print media like the New York Times, but for now, we will concentrate on how at least one-third of Americans get their 'news.'[116] I haven't left out the half of the nation who get their information from the unverified and unfiltered social networks, but that's detailed in the next chapter[117].

Back to the corporate media: profit, never patriotism, is what drives their CEOs, like the fellow at the opening of the chapter, now disgraced sexual predator Leslie Moonves. He earned $650 million between 2006 and 2018[118].

There's more. Each of these corporations comprises a twelve-person board. It may not surprise you to learn that most of them are millionaires. So it is that these seventy people decide what news Americans see every day. Then, factor in that those six corporations are primarily entertainment companies whose main profit business is movies and TV shows.

Recall, they need viewers to lure in the advertisers. So how do they get them? 'Angertainment.' That is 'stories' of murder and car chases. But they also pick up and parrot all the fake right-wing BS that Trump and far-right media pump out. For the 'news,' chaos and fear mean viewers. It was Jon Stewart, speaking to Fox News (so ironic) back in 2011, who said, 'The bias of the mainstream media is towards sensationalism, conflict, and laziness.''[119]

Comedian Michelle Wolf also spoke an unpalatable truth about their enabling of Trump at the 2018 White House Correspondents Dinner;

I think what no one in this room wants to admit is that Trump has helped all of you,". "He couldn't sell steaks or vodka or water or college or ties or Eric—but he has helped you. He's helped you sell your papers and your books and your TV. You helped create this monster, and now you're profiting off of him.[120]

It wasn't always this way. As we have read, up to 1987, anyone who wanted to broadcast across the public airwaves had to ensure fair and balanced coverage, as laid down in the Fairness Doctrine of 1949[121]. Just to note, before 1987, there were only three terrestrial TV channels: ABC, CBS, and NBC.

Back in the post-World War II heyday of the media, a career in TV or print journalism was considered something to aspire to, and standards were high. Journalists knew the prestige and responsibility of what is known as the Fourth Estate; the free press sitting alongside the legislative, executive and judicial branches in any democracy. Its purpose was and is to hold power to account.

So it was up to 1987 that true television journalism shone. Essentially, Americans received vetted factual information, and most inhabited a shared reality. The transforming event would be the death of the Fairness Doctrine and the birth of cable news. From that we get CNN (launched in 1980 but only came to prominence with its wall-to-wall coverage of the first Gulf War in 1991), AM hate radio, and Fox.

Today, the corporations that own the media are aware of our evolutionary bias towards ingesting bad news. They know that, in the past, this was what would have kept our forebears from becoming snacks for bears, crocodiles, or tigers. The predators may have changed, but our brains have remained the same. Clinical psychologist Dr. Jana Scrivani summed up the corporate media business model perfectly,

They exist to make money. What do they make money on? They make money on advertisements. What do you need to make money on advertisements? You need viewers. How do you get viewers? Simple recipe; You make them really scared, you make them really angry, and then you promise them that you can make them safe, but that they have to keep tuning in, in order to keep themselves safe. The 'Rage Machine' is such a great term for it. It's just churning; fear, rage, and the promise of relief, over and over again. That spills over into our perception of reality.[122]

Going back to the TV news' addiction to spectacle, I could also intertwine that with thirty-one years of (anti) 'reality TV' shows. Much of it is made by the same corporations that bring you your news. Take 'Cops,' a show that ran between 1989 and 2020 and was produced by Rupert Murdoch's Fox network[123]. Here we have real-life footage, hyper-edited to render it almost fiction-like—which is the paradox of 'reality TV.' Nonetheless, in this popular show, ordinary citizens got to see mostly black men being arrested. From that, biases against black men would have been reinforced, and viewers would have imagined life was pretty unsafe.

Thus we see the sad irony of violent crime being cut in half across most of America since 'Cops' was first aired[124], yet people see so much 'real' crime on the TV, whether on the news or on reality TV, that they think America is a very dangerous place.

This dovetails into police malpractice. Voters think cops must be under constant attack, so they vote in politicians who approve big-budget increases for the police and prisons. This disproportionately affects people of color. In 2024, it ensured that thousands weren't able to vote Democratic to stop gun violence, keep abortion legal, slow down global warming, and save democracy.

America is exceptional in the high-income world for having for-profit news. Canada, Australia, and most countries in Europe have taxpayer-funded impartial public broadcasters to provide factual news. In England, for a hundred years, there has been the British Broadcasting Corporation. It needs no advertising because it is taxpayer-funded, and as part of its charter, it is legally required to provide balanced, impartial information[125].

The BBC gets beaten up by both sides, with the left thinking that they are too right-wing and most on the right wanting to neuter them. But, on balance, having an unbiased public broadcaster is quite a good predictor of a stable society. After all, that's what America had until 1987.

We have seen that Trump knew the secret of forcing the media to pay attention to him; he just did endless outrageous things. Steve Bannon called it "flooding the zone with shit[126]." He's not original. The Russians have been at it for years; they call it the "Firestorm of Falsehood."[127]

It works like this. On social media, right-wing propagandists scream fake BS about CRT, DEI, 'woke,' trans folks, Hunter Biden's laptop, or Haitians eating pets. This is then picked up and amplified by the Murdoch Misinformation Machine, Fox News. All this keeps the corporate media on the boil, excited and distracted by the latest nonsense. As we have seen, the media, ever hungry for ratings, are content to be semi-compliant partners.

This leads us on to the media's idea of itself as an impartial observer and reporter of the facts. There is a concept known as 'false equivalence.' In this, two arguments receive the same weight and are treated as equally credible[128]. It matters not that one argument may be full of lies. As an example, for the whole of the Biden presidency, polls showed Americans believing that the nation was in a recession, the stock market was down, and unemployment was high[129]. Much of this can be traced back to right-wing lies reported by the media as facts, reinforcing public sentiment of a poor economy[130].

False equivalence takes us on to another corrosive aspect of how the television and print media failed Americans and smoothed the way for Trump to win in 2024. Journalist Parker Molloy coined the superb phrase 'sanewashing.'[131] The media did so much of this that many Americans didn't understand the authoritarianism revealing itself before their very own eyes. To those who paid attention, Trump's speeches were riddled with dozens of lies, errors, and brain malfunctions that, if voters knew, may have caused them to question his competence or sanity. Yet, unlike Joe Biden's solitary gaffes that had journalists demanding he drop out of the presidential race, almost every corporate news outlet and major newspaper either corrected Trump's lies and errors or glossed over them.

It's not just Trump who receives the gift of double standards either. Despite their members grooming children, having rapists in their fold, and using Hitler quotes, The New York Times calls 'Moms for Liberty' a "run-of-the-mill conservative group of moms."[132]

In North Carolina, Mark Robinson, the black lieutenant governor and 2024 GOP gubernatorial candidate, denied the Holocaust, praised Hitler, thought women shouldn't vote, equated civil rights to slavery, and worried more about the rights of AR-15 owners than the rights of living Americans who don't want to die by an AR-15. Suffice to say, he denied the results of the 2020 election and was boosted by Trump. Despite all this, The New York Times gently sanewashed Robinson by describing him as a 'political firebrand.'[133]

This segues us back to the corporate media's love of seeing 'both sides' of everything and false equivalence. As an example, back in 2023, we found out Trump had stolen more highly classified documents than notorious traitors Aldrich Ames and Robert Hansen combined[134]. It wouldn't even have been a story if, when asked by the National Archives to return them, he had done so. Instead, he claimed the documents were his (rather than belonging to the United States of America.)

After being asked repeatedly to return them and refusing, finally the FBI liaised with the Secret Service to conduct a search of Mar-a-Lago while Trump was away. They found box loads of classified docs, including nuclear secrets, many stored in an unsecured toilet for any of the foreign agents milling around to find. After that, Trump, Fox News, and elected Republicans accused the FBI of a 'political witch-hunt,' and one Confederate Taliban terrorist was shot dead after he went to an FBI field office to kill their agents[135].

Around the same time, President Biden's office contacted the National Archives to return some documents of low-level information that would have been mistakenly packed up when he left the Obama White House. There were no histrionics and no demonizing of the FBI. Yet, the media covered both stories as if they were the same[136].

Here, I must offer a caveat. Many political reporters did and do know the terrible mechanics of what's going on. However, out of fear of losing their jobs, they trade access to right-wing politicians in return for suppressing the unsavory information about those politicians.

For other journalists who knew everything, especially before the 2020 election, they didn't bother telling us how bad things really were because they were busy securing their multi-million-dollar book deals. Instead, we had to wait until their books came out—after the election—to learn everything[137].

Apart from propping up the GOP to maintain the facade of the horse race, there is another truth of why they smash down on Democrats yet treat Republicans with kid gloves. It is the same reason GOP politicians bow down to Trump and his cult. They are terrified that a radicalized MAGA terrorist might come into their offices and start shooting or stalk them at their homes. As craven as these hacks are, they have enough general intelligence to know a supersonic round from an AR-15 or a close contact wound from a nine-millimeter pistol is a damn sight more dangerous than a meek liberal bleating about 'media balance.'

As for that meek liberal. It's a mistake to think that the media needs to be treated with civility and deference. So it is that when they lie, they need to be shouted at and shouted down. I recall Driftglass of the Professional Left podcast suggesting that liberals start calling out lazy reporters with lines like 'Why do you hate America so much?' and 'Why are you always parroting Republican lies and fake news?'[138] Then, in their shock, they will start reporting the facts. Paradoxically, this is not because they love balance or democracy, but because friction—even when it is aimed against them—is great for ratings and clicks, which means profits, which is all they are interested in.

At this point, I'm going to improve your life by showing how to separate lies from the truth. Indeed, that's half the battle of being a critical thinker. I will give you a four-step fail-safe method anyone can use to spot fake news and make themselves much smarter.

However, first, we must understand two terms. The first is misinformation; this could be a mistake, such as someone getting a fact wrong, like telling you the moon is 250 million miles away when it is, in fact, only 250,000 miles away.

Then, there is disinformation. It is there to deliberately and maliciously disinform you, like someone telling you the moon isn't actually there; it's just a Deep State manufactured illusion. Disinformation covers everything that comes out of Trump's mouth.

Now to the four-step process. First, alarm bells should always ring if the source is "punching down and kissing up." If they are demeaning or railing against someone less powerful than themselves, like people of color, LGBTQ+ people, low-income folks, immigrants, or liberal women, that's a big flashing neon sign.

Thus, if you're watching someone bullying the bullied, you know you're dealing with one of the devil's winged monkeys. Invariably, these fiends always kiss up to their masters like Trump or Putin. This rule applies to almost everyone on the far-right. Just to note, 'Miss Anne' style, right-wing women, such as Megan Kelly, Marjorie Taylor Greene, and Ann Coulter, always punch down and kiss up, acting in blissful complicity as useful idiots for the patriarchy.

Second, when you come across 'punching down and kissing up' plus 'outrage,' it is a dead cert guarantee of fake news. Alex Jones, Tucker Carlson, Steve Bannon, Fox News, Newsmax and all far-right podcasters do it. Contrast all of them with the British BBC, NPR, or any of those sources at the bottom of the chapter, who never punch down or engage in hate speech.

Third, be very leery of any 'news' that attacks, or is outraged at, peer-accepted authoritative sources like doctors, scientists, or teachers. Also, if the source is more outraged at the people fighting racism than at the racists, that's a warning sign. If LGBTQ+ folks are more troubling than the people who attack LGBTQ+ folks, again, a warning. If they are more concerned about 'gun rights' than the rights of citizens to be safe from guns, once again, it's a warning. And, if they talk about the fetus while ignoring the rights of women, you know you're dealing with a critically bad actor.

Finally, there's the kicker. When watching, listening to, or reading news that criticizes a liberal, just ask yourself the question, "What would they say if Trump (or any Republican) did it?"

I will spin it around for you. Just consider if Joe Biden had four separate criminal trials pending, had been convicted of fraud, stolen classified documents, quoted Adolf Hitler, hosted foreign autocrats, sided with Russia over NATO, used the US government as a piggy bank, mocked wounded veterans, paid off an adult film star, caused the deaths of over four hundred thousand Americans, proposed locking up his opponents, tried to stage a coup, and announced he wanted to become a dictator. Do you think that the media might have reported it a little differently?

Of course, it always helps to get your information from truthful sources. Here are some sources I've used to write this book and to help me think the way I do. There is the BBC, NPR, Huffington Post, Slate, Mother

Jones, The Daily Beast, The Guardian, ProPublica, Salon, Rolling Stone, and Vox. These outlets report on objective facts and truth.

Also, there are independent media podcasts that ensure it's impossible to be dumb if you listen to them. Shows like The Daily Beans, The Bob Cesca Show, Tell Me Everything, Majority 54, The New Abnormal, The Stephanie Miller Show, The Mehdi Hassan Show, The Hal Sparks Radio Program, The Professional Left podcast, On Democracy, The Muckrake Podcast, and Democracy-ish.

Chapter 7

The Tech Bros Doomsday Machines Really Are Coming To Kill You

Imagine if social media hadn't been invented, and in 2023, someone came to Shark Tank with this:

> We propose to start a social network that can link billions of people together, whilst being completely unregulated. Our network will specialize in providing users with unchecked and unverified information as if it were truth. The network will operate 24 hours a day, 365 days a year to spread fear, hate, and misinformation. It will make users angry, depressed, and scared, while teaching them how to kill themselves and others. The network will allow our enemies a back door to attack America without ever having to send one missile or soldier. The result of all this is our guarantee that within ten years of launch, the network will be ready to collapse American democracy.

Any clown pitching this idea would be shown the door without too much haste and certainly wouldn't get funding. However, I forgot to include the most important part of the pitch:

But it will make us and our investors tens of billions of dollars
in profits, every year.

In 1996, the World Wide Web had only existed for three years; Netflix was a mail-order DVD company. The first Google search wouldn't be until two years later; Facebook was eight years away (its founder, Mark Zuckerberg, was still only twelve years old), and the first 'tweet' wouldn't be sent until ten years later.

1996 was also the year that the Clinton Administration, ushered along by libertarian right-wing interests, passed the 1996 Communications Decency Act. Section 230 of the Act stated:

No provider or user of an interactive computer service shall
be treated as the publisher or speaker of any information
provided by another information content provider.[139]

The point is that, in 1996, no one could imagine how democracy-threateningly powerful these companies would become.

Twitter was sold to Mad Musk in 2022 for $44 billion, the same value as the Ford Motor Company. But that's just a minnow compared to the sharks. In 2024, Meta, at $1.2 trillion, is worth as much as the annual GDP of Switzerland[140]. Then we get to Alphabet (Google), whose value at $1.8 trillion is within touching distance of the whole Canadian economy[141].

How did they get this way? Well, we made them. At the outset, social media and search engines were products without any ability to earn a profit. It's mainly because we were too cheap to pay for Facebook, Google, or Twitter, so these corporations just gave their apps away for free.

It would be a few years before luck came calling and showed them how to make money from people discussing TV shows and posting cat videos. Their serendipitous moment came around in 2008 with the launch of the iPhone (and other smartphones) that allowed us to walk around with the internet in our pockets.

Once the phone became our conjoined companion, we had done most of their work for them. Now, with people spending so much time glued to the screen (in Big Tech parlance, that's 'Time On Device' or TOD[142]), a bankrupt business model became a golden goose.

By utilizing the personal information that we users gave them, the originally innocently designed algorithms would become the most efficient binary sorting machines in human history, especially useful for filtering us into identity groups.

With the algorithms biased towards maximizing users' TOD, it just so happened the most effective way of ensuring that was to use the two most primal methods of garnering attention, fear, and anger[143].

By making both sides scared of and angry towards the other side, our evolutionary instincts would lean towards survival, which meant, for our own survival, we'd never be able to look away. So were born the enragement/engagement Doomsday Machines, which prioritize hate and rage over moderation and nuance.

The old phrase "If you're not paying for it, then you're the product" became true. By turning their users into a commodity, they could sell our data (us) to their advertisers. So it is that today Facebook, Google, and Twitter earn over 80% of their revenue from advertising[144].

Going back to 1996, do you really imagine lawmakers would have called these 'Doomsday Machines' platforms rather than publishers, had they known what their algorithms would be promoting and pushing in 2023?

- COVID-19 is a hoax.

- 9/11 was a US government plot to ......

- Vaccines will kill you.

- The Holocaust never happened

- The Jews control the world

- The 2020 election was stolen

Yet, just look on Twitter or Facebook to find millions of lies like these. These engines of radicalization allow modern-day lie-peddlers and chaos agents like Musk and Trump to broadcast devilishly anti-progress ideas—all with no fact-checking—instantly and directly to the screens of millions, or even hundreds of millions, of people.

Before we continue, just a quick note on the Silicon Valley founders myth. I'm thinking of billionaire oligarchs like Mark Zuckerberg and Mark Andreesen. These characters offer a story of how they did it all on their own, with no help.

Let's just examine that story. The government invented the internet using your grandparents' tax dollars in 1969[145]. The World Wide Web Graphical User Interface, which allows us to look up those cat videos, gun videos, and more salacious fare, was invented in 1989 in the French government-run CERN laboratories, using European taxpayers' monies[146]. The GPS that allows everything to work on the move, again, paid for by your grandparents' taxes in 1978.

The point is the creators of the social networks did nothing. They just freeloaded off clever government workers and your grandparents' taxes, all while pretending, with the fawning complicity of the idiotic corporate media, that they are the be-all and end-all of humanity. Indeed, if we are to believe them, without their absolute magnificence, we would all crumble and die.

The truth of the matter is this. If most of the tech bros' invasive social media apps disappeared tomorrow, the world would be a much happier, much saner, and just as productive a place.

Also, without social media, something quite magical would happen: you'd be interacting with lots of real people, exactly what human beings were meant to do—not staring at a soulless screen.

But that's another future. Today, in Facebook and WhatsApp, Mark Zuckerberg knows he has created a doomsday machine that can spread propaganda around the world faster than a KGB agent strapped to the back of a cruise missile. For any bad actors wanting to start a riot, a genocide, or even kill a democracy, Facebook's algorithm is a willing partner. You want receipts? It enabled a genocide in Myanmar way back in 2012[147]. Then, in the 2016 US election, it did next to nothing to stop Russian disinformation from influencing nearly thirty million Americans[148], and by 2020, Facebook had become a full-time misinformation machine to promote right-wing propaganda[149].

Then there's Twitter, especially under its self-radicalized bawling billionaire owner, Mad Musk, which actively promotes neo-Nazi and other far-right content. Indeed, Musk makes no pretense about his disdain for democracy and his support for Trump[150]. As for Instagram, unfortunately, it just makes people sad, sufficiently so sometimes to want to kill themselves[151].

I could include Google here, which owns YouTube, a site ideal for searching out brain cell-sapping disinformation videos, bomb-making videos, and beheading videos. Studies have shown that YouTube actively sets out to harm users by steering them to the most dangerous content[152].

All this being said, I don't believe for one minute that the creators of Facebook, Twitter, or YouTube intended their platforms would become what they are. However, the minor fixes that would have turned them into happy online communities would have cost the billionaire owners of these corporations some of their profits and wealth.

That is unacceptable to them. So, it is today that these mind melting mothafuckers murder their users' (victims?) minds to keep the cash rolling in. Evil is a powerful word, but I'm sure that before 2040, historians will look back and know exactly what to call them. For today, if you want advice on how to protect yourself against the doomsday machines, there's this;

> I don't generally want my kids to be sitting in front of a TV
> or a computer for a long period of time.[153]

Those could be words of a frumpy old professor or an outdoorsman. Instead, it's 'doomsday machine' creator Mark Zuckerberg telling us in 2019 how, in private, he does exactly the opposite of what his algorithms make you do.

If you want to know the year that the world changed indelibly, it was 2012. That was the year the smartphone consummated its marriage to social media. Even though Facebook and Twitter had been around for at least four years, they could only be accessed on a clunky laptop or PC. However, once people could find them on their phones, the phone became an extension of their own bodies.

Never kid yourself about the world before 2012. It was a much more patriarchal, unstable, and violent place. For receipts, the 1960s gave us the anti-civil rights violence, the Cuban Missile Crisis, and the Vietnam War. And John Kennedy, Dr. Martin Luther King Jr., Malcolm X, and Robert Kennedy were all assassinated in that decade. Yet Americans lived in more or less a shared reality, getting their news and information from similar fact-based sources.

Then spin through the 1970s, where terror and political violence flourished in rich countries. In Britain, France, Germany, Italy, and Spain, it was normal for terrorist movements to detonate bombs in civilian areas. Then, throughout the 1980s, the world lived under the threat of the Cold War sword of Damocles—nuclear annihilation. Despite this, our grasp of facts and reality was still solid.

In the 1990s, elections would (aside from Bush 43) go smoothly, and science was, on the whole, accepted. Republicans helped fix the hole in the ozone layer and even allowed the EPA to force fossil fuel companies to put pollution scrubbers on power stations to stop acid rain. Even guns were kept in check, with semi-automatic rifles banned for ten years. Anti-vaccination people were there, but were mostly festering in the darkest recesses of the nascent internet; ditto, Holocaust deniers and 'Jew' haters.

Even after 9/11, quite a lot of progress happened without that much fuss. Never forget that AM hate-radio stochastic terrorists like Rush Limbaugh had been poisoning and radicalizing American minds since 1988, and Fox 'News' had been spewing out hate on the TV since 1996. Yet, despite all that hate, we still moved forward, with Barack Obama getting elected twice.

Then we hit that Genesis moment in 2012. That year, there were 680 million smartphones sold worldwide, but by 2014, it had doubled to 1.2 billion, mostly in the high-income world[154]. Facebook users, in a symbiotic partnership, shot up from 12 million in 2006 to 1 billion in 2012[155]. This was the point where many people left the shared factual reality and entered an Alice in Wonderland world, where they could believe "as many as six impossible things before breakfast."[156]

Back in 2012, a certain Donald Trump, who up to then simply coveted the thought of being invited to New York high-society parties, used Twitter mostly for gossip and self-promotion. However, in his putrid and sociopathic mind, hatred was always a fellow dark traveler. From 2012, he ramped up his 'political' use of Twitter to tweet to the 167 million users in 2012.[157]

We know that one of Trump's greatest 'skills' is to get people to look at him so that he can monetize his 'brand.' He understood that by using this new media, his depraved and demonic thoughts could bypass the fact-checkers and smoothing filters of the mainstream media. He needn't have worried, for the media were so greedy for ratings, his tweets only got them to focus on him even more.

Always remember, Trump's con was to project an image of a successful national figure from "Celebrity Apprentice." In 2016, I knew people who believed that he was successful just because he was the 'CEO' on that TV show. They, like many, couldn't separate 'reality' from real.

Nonetheless, Twitter allowed him to get his unfiltered, unverified, un-challenged views across; indeed, the more outrageous, the better, such as this gem from August 2012:

> An 'extremely credible source' has called my office and told me that @BarackObama's birth certificate is a fraud.[158]

So unoriginal is he that even in that tweet, the *'extremely credible source'* is himself. For reference, throughout the 1970s and up to the 1990s, he would pretend to be his own PR man. Using names like "John Miller" and "John Barron," he'd phone up journalists claiming to *'have stories about Trump.'*[159] His use of Twitter simply allowed him to update the means of communication and ditch the fake PR guy.

Later, in 2012, we can watch his continued evolution from fool to fascist. Here, after President Obama's second victory, without a single scintilla of proof, is the foundation for his 'big lie' about the presidential election in 2020.

> This election is a total sham and a travesty. We are not a democracy! — Donald J. Trump[160]

He also recognized a ready constituency in the anti-vaccination dis-ease-spreaders, many of whom would later provide useful and willing fodder for QAnon:

Healthy young child goes to doctor, gets pumped with massive shot of many vaccines, doesn't feel good and changes - AUTISM. Many such cases![161]

Just look at his words, *"Many such cases!"* All set to terrify low-information people. Tweets like this would set him up to look like an honest broker who 'tells it like it is' and was 'authentic.'

This moves us on to one of the best examples of the doomsday machines being explained. It comes from a man in England named 'Mizzy.' To garner our attention, this 'social media content creator' recorded himself doing outrageous things that could (and did) get him arrested. He then posted the videos on Twitter and TikTok[162]. For our purposes, there was one video in which he walks, uninvited, into strangers' homes and plonks himself down on their sofas while recording the owner's reaction[163].

His mindset was summed up in an interview with the London Independent newspaper and seems perfectly aligned with what the social media companies' algorithms are set up for;

He started to realize that every time he "upped the ante and did wilder videos" he would garner more online engagement – so that is what he continued to do.

Nonetheless, Mizzy hit the nail on the head for both social media (and corporate media) when he said,

Literally, hate brings money, hate brings likes, hate brings views. It doesn't matter – love or hate, it still brings views ... It's not like I prefer to do the hateful stuff, it's just easier to do the hateful stuff.[164]

This is the social media business model in a nutshell. It is predicated on getting users glued to their screens, meaning engagement. Crazier content, whether from Mizzy, Alex Jones, or Donald Trump, allows the social media companies to hook more viewers to sell more advertising, which leads to more profits. More profits mean more power, and more power means they can stymie any future regulation.

When, in 1996, the Clinton Administration gave the "Interactive Computer Services" a pass on regulation, it couldn't have known how they would turn into unverified cesspits of misinformation and disinformation. And they couldn't have conceived how the algorithms would prey on our basest instincts to be fearful and angry.

At this point, I can hear people speaking of the benefits of social media. They might point to the grandmas who can see their grandkids and kids who can post selfies, or folks showing us pictures of their dinner. Okay, that's a little facetious, because social media did allow marginalized people to see themselves and for women to shine a spotlight on sex offenders with #METOO.

However, weigh that up against the fact that Russia has, since 2016, weaponized Facebook to subvert US democracy, and how TikTok is an instrument of the Chinese Communist Party, and Twitter is run by Russia's most useful (unpaid) idiot. Then there are the anti-vaccine lies that metamorphosized into COVID lies that were amplified and spread on social media to kill millions around the world.

As for women, look at the vast number of Andrew Tate-style characters of the 'manosphere' who have proliferated to preach pure misogyny to disaffected young men. So it is that today groomed junior patriarchs who used to talk about 'picking women up' now speak of making them 'compliant'.

Social media is also the chatroom for all the white supremacist 'accelerationists,' dreaming of civil wars, societal breakdowns, and the world being rebuilt in their image, with them on top and everyone else subordinate. The precursors of this are the terrorists and mass shooters, each groomed and radicalized against another, whether black, brown, Jewish, or LGBTQ people. Next to none of this would have happened without the social networks or YouTube.

Facebook, Twitter, and YouTube are willingly compliant partners in helping to murder American democracy. It is on these platforms that the far-right disinformation is amplified and dispersed into the world by patriarchal multi-millionaire social media podcasters like Dan Bongino, Tim Pool, and Joe Rogan.

Just a point to note. If liberals think things can't get worse, imagine the avalanche of fake AI stories and videos that will be promoted by Musk, Zuckerberg, and the far-right podcasters over the next few years to fool and radicalize low-information people.

The solution to all this is regulation to turn the social media corporations into publishers rather than platforms. As far as that regulation goes, a lot of time is being wasted on trying to figure out how to repeal or override the Section 230 exemption that affords these social media corporations effective immunity. We know that today, a "provider of an interactive computer service" cannot be treated as the publisher or speaker of third-party content. However, this is not a problem, as Section 230 lawmakers kindly defined what an 'Interactive Service Provider' is;

> "any information service, system, or access software provider
> that provides or enables computer access by multiple users to
> a computer server."[165]

Note the singular "server", as it's vital. There's one shown below.

You may wonder how we are going to work out what a server is. Thankfully, the job has been done for us. If you want to buy a server, just go to a computer hardware supplier. I went to Dell, one of the world's leading supplier of servers. This is a $100,000 'server' from Dell. It can store nearly 400 terabytes of data; That's twenty thousand hours of HD movies[166].

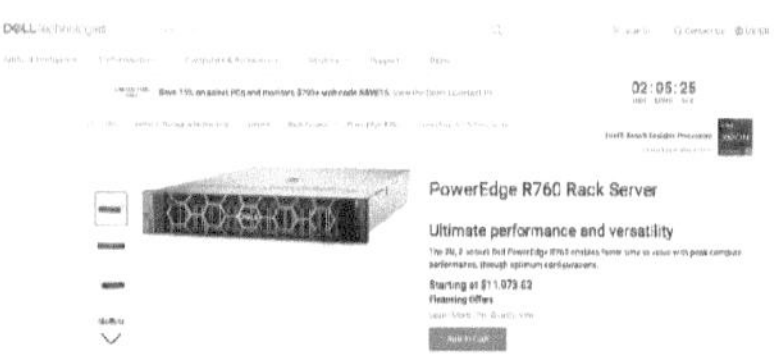

Remember, Dell will only sell you one 'server' for your $100,000, not one hundred thousand.

To understand how this affects the social media corporations, we can look at Meta, the owners of Facebook. Today, they have twenty-two data centers (once called 'server farms') around the world[167]. Each one of these, built-for-Artificial Intelligence, fake-news spewing, energy-guzzling (set to consume one-tenth of all US energy over the next couple of years[168]), planet heating[169]data centres are around the size of thirty football fields and costs billions of dollars. They look like the image below, with tens of thousands of 'servers' in each location. In the image, each 'rack' holds twelve individual servers[170].

If we follow the letter of the regulation, all single 'server' small businesses and start-ups are 'Interactive Computer Services,' but, overnight, Meta, Google, and Twitter, with their gargantuan data centers containing tens of thousands of servers, all become publishers, just like Fox 'News.'

Now that Big Tech is no longer covered by Section 230, the class action lawyers of America can sue them for their lies, or the lies they promote. Thus, when the networks promote suicide, they get sued. When they promote gun violence, they get sued, and when they promote election lies, they get sued.

The list just keeps on growing. If you've been a victim of fake influencers, or crypto con men, you can sue. If the algorithm stoked violence that led to your town being burnt down, you can sue, and if their algorithms allowed you to be radicalized, you can sue.

Watch how, miraculously, in order to avoid lawsuits, these social media companies adapt their algorithms to clamp down on the inflammatory, born-to-lie grifters like Tucker Carlson, Alex Jones, and Andrew Tate.

Just to note. A test case will end up at the Supreme Court, where the six high priests—who appointed themselves experts in everything—will muddy the waters to allow the exemption. Don't let them. After all, the singular and the plural are first-grade simple to understand.

To this point, traditionally, nice, well-meaning liberal lawyers have appeared before the Supreme Court, bowed down and argued meekly, and before we know it, we have Citizens United, Shelby County and Heller; Those would be cases that gave us unlimited money in politics, unlimited voter suppression and unlimited guns.

If I may offer some unsolicited advice. Those three cases were lost because ordinary people of all political persuasions weren't involved in them. It's the same for the 2022 Dobbs ruling that criminalized abortion. Only liberals wanted to save women's rights. However, being a victim of the algorithms is not a Democratic or Republican issue. It affects people in both red and blue states, and rural and urban areas. After all, there must be millions of MAGA-hat-wearing Trump supporters in Florida, Texas or Tennessee who have suffered devastating mental damage because of his lies.

With them on board, it becomes an unstoppable movement. Small-town lawyers and big city lawyers will sign up red and blue folks to join the actions. This 'people power' is a vitally important aspect of the case. So it is, before the case even gets to the Supreme Court, people will know they are entitled to cash. With the prospect of $5,000 or $10,000 in damages as their incentive, rough, tough red state folks will not let demented abortion-banning, machine gun-legalizing hacks like Alito, Roberts and Thomas deny them what is rightfully theirs. And I can assure you that Sam, John and Clarence are a damn sight more worried by a gun-owning rural Pennsylvanian than they are of an EV-driving, latte-sipping, coastal liberal.

That's the self-interested secret to winning the case; lawyers who want to win and citizens who want cash.

Chapter 8

The Silence Of The LAMB's And The Stupidity Of Elon Musk.

By the end of the chapter, you will have learned about the greatest threat facing workers that politicians of all stripes will not talk about, but also a solution to stop it from happening.

Before we get to that, we have to address the people who are coming for your jobs. Over the next few pages, I will reveal not only how dumb billionaire job-killers are but also how dangerous they are.

Today, many people have been gaslit into admiring the 'intellect' of Elon Musk. This conveniently ignores the fact that most of his legion of predictions are wrong—whether that COVID-19 would only infect 35,000 people, that a recession would come in 2022, 2023 and 2024, that Ron DeSantis could be president in 2024, or that there would a new civil war, etc.

This brings us on to 'rent-seeking' Musk's first love: Mars. Today, he is at the forefront of those who want to grift us for billions of tax dollars to travel to the Red Planet. He asserts humans could land on Mars within four years and be living there within twenty years[171]. All of this is calmly being taken at face value by most of the media. So let's examine the idea.

Mars is about one hundred and forty million miles away[172]. We know how hard it is to get an *unmanned* probe to the Moon, and that's 'only' two hundred and fifty thousand miles away. Flying to Mars is equivalent to flying five hundred and sixty Moon missions in one go. This is from

NASA scientist Dr. Michelle Thaller, speaking to the US Sun newspaper about Musk's dream;

> It's possible he wouldn't make it that far because of the radiation in space between here and Mars._If the Sun has a big solar flare or a big ejection of material that happens quite commonly, that would kill him.[173]

Still, assume that miracles happen, and humans actually get to the Red Planet, then they would spend hours each day donning their spacesuits as they are now in a place with no oxygen. In fact, it's worse; Mars' atmosphere is 96% carbon dioxide. That would be the same Co2, of which a tiny change over the past sixty years, from 0.03% to 0.04% of the Earth's atmosphere, is suffocating us today[174].

Few people also know that on Mars, the nighttime temperature reaches a rather uninviting -284 degrees Fahrenheit (winters in Alaska seldom get colder than -30 F). Then, there's this gem from NASA in 2022;

> A large dust storm on Mars, nearly twice the size of the United States, covered the southern hemisphere of the Red Planet in early January 2022, leading to some of NASA's explorers on the surface hitting pause on their normal activities. NASA's Insight Lander put itself in a "safe mode" to conserve battery power after dust prevented sunlight from reaching the solar panels.[175]

It can take weeks for the dust clouds to settle after these storms. Just remember that everything on Mars will work from solar power, and for solar panels to convert the sun's rays into energy, first they need to see the sun.

If this hasn't put you off, have a look at Mars. It's an arid desert wasteland where no fruit, vegetables or crops could ever grow.

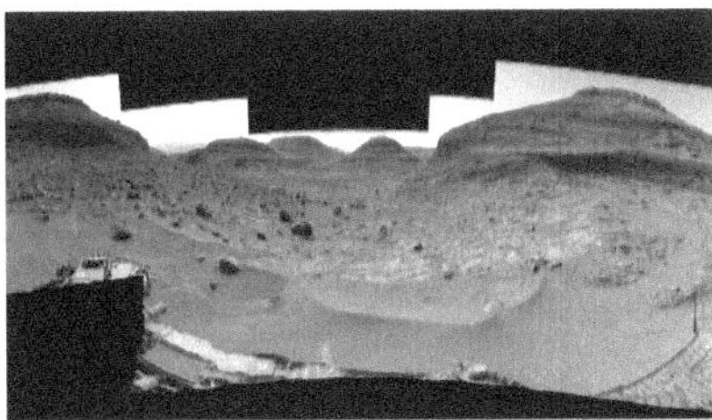

The barren landscape means there won't be any of Earth's majestic oceans, rivers, streams, forests, or mountains. So you can forget about seeing another stunning sunrise or sunset, or going to the park or the beach with your friends.

Of course, no nature means no animals; no birds, cats, dogs, sheep, deer, wolves, elephants, or giraffes...you get the point. If humans ever get to that desolate dust bowl, sadly, they will find they couldn't have invented a better place to make people want to commit suicide.

Oh, and NASA's own estimate for the cost of this Martian flight of fancy? A piddling half a trillion of your tax dollars[176].

As if all that wasn't enough, Google DeepMind co-founder Dr. Demis Hassabis questioned Mad Musk back in 2012, long before people were talking about AI and its potential threats to humanity. Dr. Hassabis explained to the man-baby how the same super intelligent AI that Musk was worried about ending human life on Earth (even though, in 2024, his engineers have released their own AI[177] could follow us from Earth to

Mars[178]. Mad Musk went speechless. Bear all of this in mind, as we will return to this fool and his 'ideas' later.

Back here on Earth, we get to meet the employees of another gentleman who dreams of going into space: Amazon's billionaire boss, Jeff Bezos. For her 2019 book, "On the Clock", author Emily Guendelsberger recounted her experience of working in Jeff's Orwellian-sounding, Amazon Fulfillment Centre SDF8,

> When you clock in at Amazon, the first thing you do is grab a scan gun—a bit like a scanner you'd see at the grocery, but with an LCD screen that tells you what task to do next and starts counting down the seconds you have left to do it. It also tracks your location by GPS—and you take it everywhere with you, even the bathroom. Failure to stay ahead of the countdown—to make rate—was grounds for termination, regardless of why.[179]

This is all in the service of making workers more 'efficient.' At what, you may ask? Well, making sure you get your next-day Prime delivery. Amazon workers were lifting heavy boxes up and down stairs and walking up to fifteen miles a day in a factory the size of twenty football fields. For their labor, they could expect back problems, knee problems, and wrist problems.

That's no problem for Jeff. Being all about 'efficiency,' he knew it was cheaper to install painkiller machines dispensing Tylenol and Advil rather than have his workers queuing up at the warehouse's AMCARE infirmary[180]. It was simple economics: less time spent in the infirmary means more time to work.

Let's not kid ourselves that low-paid, repetitive, and zero-autonomy work is anything to celebrate. However, things can be worse. When people think of the future of work, many imagine robots in factories replacing workers. These aren't new thoughts. Back in 1965, NATO suggested replacing their test pilots with machines. Albert Scott Crossfield, a pilot, asked the question;

> Where can you find another non-linear servo-mechanism weighing only 150 pounds and having great adaptability, that can be produced so cheaply by completely unskilled labor?[181]

Today's billionaire oligarchs have no time for such romantic notions. Thus, even while the human machines are hard at work, people like Jeff are searching for the perfect robot to replace them. The uber-capitalist knows the robot can do more work in less time and at a lower cost than any human. It's already starting, and videos are available online showing robot handlers at the Amazon factory[182].

These machines are both amazing and frightening. They never get back-aches, need time off, or require wages, so as far as productivity and savings go, they are going to hit it out of the park for Jeff and his stockholders. This is all in the service of our getting those 'Prime' deliveries even faster, but at what human cost? It was the leadership guru, Warren Bennis, who quipped;

> The factory of the future will have only two employees, a man
> and a dog. ... The dog will be there to stop the man touching
> the equipment.[183]

It led me to think of the three and a half million truck drivers in America. Trucking is one of the last decent-paying jobs that non-college-educated (mostly) men can get[184].

Alas, even they aren't safe from the robots. In 2024, self-driving trucks may be just a few Christmases away, which that means goodbye to the trucker, and goodness only knows what they do for a living then.

This dystopia comes with one small proviso: for some time, the robo-truck will still need a human in the driving seat, acting as a failsafe. Their job will be to navigate the complicated last few miles to the depot or hub. Unfortunately, in 'teaching' the truck how to mimic that last task, the human becomes complicit in ensuring their own redundancy.

This reminds me of a five-minute Vice News video[185] on YouTube that future historians can use as reference material when they ponder where all the jobs went. It shows a TuSimple autonomous truck driving itself on Arizona roads in 2019. The video then cuts to the vice president of the company sitting down with three independent owner-operator truckers in a diner.

To begin, the drivers seem pretty confident and relaxed. They ask him all the right questions, such as, "How does it handle being cut off in traffic?" and "How does it handle high winds?" and "What's it like with weight in the trailer?" These are questions from the weeds that only the most seasoned truckers would know to ask. The drivers may have been expecting to catch the VP out and send him scurrying back to his skunk works to spend another ten years trying to make the AI cope with the intricate task of hauling 80,000 lbs of goods safely around America. Instead, the Veep smiles as he explains that the truck manages it all without a problem.

Whilst we are watching this, we get to see everything about elite merito-cratic America. The reporter is enthusiastic to talk about how wonderful the experience was, and the vice president, while perfectly pleasant, is completely oblivious to the consequences of his future job decimator. For the viewer, though, if one pays attention, they can see that the truckers just aren't expecting the answers that come back. The VP has another line: "In the future, when it's fully tested, and we don't need to have a driver in there..."

Those seventeen words are the metaphorical heavyweight boxer's knock-out punch. Hearing them is when the dawning realization of their future obsolescence hits these truckers, and they go silent. But inside their heads, they must be wondering what they will do for work, and how they will pay their truck loan, and their mortgage, and what will happen to their families?[186]

One could just leave thinking about it there, but the picture is so much bigger. If we zoom out a little, we see all the ancillary jobs that truckers help maintain. There are forty thousand truck stops across North America serving the long-distance hauler[187]. What about the chefs and waitresses at the diners where the truckers eat? Or the admin staff, cashiers, janitors, and other workers who are employed not just in the diners, but also in the movie theaters, churches, and casinos that are in some of these truck stops? Robo-Truck doesn't eat, doesn't watch movies, doesn't pray, and doesn't gamble, so that's tens of thousands of jobs gone, mostly in rural areas.

There is a quote from sociologist Richard Florida, part of which I first read in Thomas Frank's 'Listen Liberal': "The creative class anticipates the future while the working class is, in many senses, seeking protection from it. ..."[188]

The Democratic Party was supposed to protect workers, and as they haven't, some of them listen to fake-populists like Trump. Astute readers know he doesn't care. His four years in office showed all he wanted to do was make him and his wealthy donors richer with tax giveaways. His ability to get away with so much BS was because liberals, except for people like Joe Biden, Bernie Sanders, Alexandria Ocasio Cortez, and United Auto Workers president Shawn Fain, weren't offering much in the way of respite from the 'Brave New World' that Bezos, Musk, and other oligarchs have in store for us.

It isn't just blue-collar folks who are in for a shock. Ironically, the same knowledge-based-economy meritocrats who are giddily gleeful about the future may have a rude awakening. While generative artificial intelligence is terrible at being genuinely creative, both it and robotic process automation (RPA) are shockingly good at seeking patterns[189]. Now, while it is possible that, when employed as a servant to help humans, AI will allow us some huge leaps forward in food production, medicine, and science, sadly, like social media, the abundance of its use will be to harm humans.

As we read in chapter five, when I was young, I worked in the corporate finance department of what would become Lehman Brothers in London. It wasn't just investment bankers working on deals; there were also accountants, auditors, and lawyers, all engaged in the stultifyingly boring and deliriously repetitive work of pawing through the fine print of the numbers and the corporate law, looking for patterns. Of the dozens of people involved, almost all would have been earning above $100,000 in today's money.

I coined an acronym: LAMB's: Lawyers, Accountants, Management Consultants, and Bankers. These are the high-salaried, data-driven graduate and postgraduate jobs performed by meritocrats, who may well feel the heat of change just as much as a truck driver or warehouse worker. After all, if the tech bros want to introduce expensive 'robots' and pattern recognition software, then doesn't it make sense to move into the fields where they can make the most cost savings, a.k.a. 'efficiencies.'

Take corporate law. This is basically drawing up or finding loopholes in long, detailed contracts. A lot of it involves looking online for old case law. Former presidential candidate Andrew Yang wrote about his former life as a contract lawyer: "We used to joke about how much of what we did was "finding and replacing" terms in a contract."[190]

He couldn't have described a better working ground for pattern recognition software. Indeed, JP Morgan Chase has already started with COIN–Contract Intelligence. Bloomberg reported that,

> The lawyer bot or software robot works 24/7/365, is less error-prone, reviews documents in seconds, and never asks for vacation or a higher salary.[191]

We can move on to accountancy. This is nothing more than adding and subtracting numbers and knowing thousands of pages of laws and tax codes. Which again, is all about patterns.

In a similar field, there's management consultancy. All that involves is people who've never had a proper job telling people who have proper jobs how to make 'efficiencies.' Translated, this always means cost cutting or staff cuts. Again, it's just numbers and patterns. We could continue the theme of looking at redundant future careers by looking at admin jobs, insurance or marketing, but you get the idea.

One may imagine that software development must be a good way to escape the future jobs apocalypse. After all, these are the people writing the code that will put the LAMBs out of work. To give you an idea of how recently coding was considered the 'career to have,' the book, 'Coding for Dummies,' was first published in 2015. But now, AI is even coming for coding[192]. Indeed, in 2024, Google was generating a quarter of its code from AI[193].

So it is that future tech jobs are said to be in software architecture[194]. That means designing the frame of the code that will put the LAMBs out of work. However, as software projects only require a few architects, this will also make many coders redundant.

Speaking of putting people out of work, segues us back to Mad Musk. In 2023, we got a look at another part of the future that the silver-spoon-fed millionaire at birth would like when he revealed his 5 ft 8 in, 57 kg "Optimus" robot[195].

At the time, the fool had some words of 'wisdom' for American workers: "Essentially, in the future, physical work will be a choice. If you want to do it, you can, but you won't need to do it."[196]

In November 2023, Musk, speaking in the UK, as ever without journalistic (another career that AI is coming for[197]) challenge, added more musings as to when the AI will replace the need for workers, saying;

> It's hard to say exactly what that moment is, but there will come a point where no job is needed,_You can have a job if you want to have a job or sort of personal satisfaction, but the AI will be able to do everything.[198]

The meritocratic chutzpah of this unelected bawling billionaire is breathtaking. It may come as a surprise to the tone-deaf, radicalized, friendless fool that most people need to work in order to pay their bills, food, and rent.

Yet, still unaware of his own mediocrity and with no supporting data or evidence, he threw out that the future will be a time of "universal high income."[199] Tell that to the unemployed LAMBs, truckers, or warehouse workers.

It's not that the tech bros don't have a plan for workers; they do: the government must pay a universal basic income (UBI). No corporate media journalists ever talk about it, but the cost of just 10% of the US workforce (twenty million workers) receiving a $15,000 UBI each year is a mere trifle at $300 billion.

Obviously, it's too much to expect lazy, fawning journalists to ask a few questions of these oligarchs, so I'll help them along with, "What's your vision of employment in the future?" and "How are the laid-off workers going to afford to live without wages?" Some deeper questions could be, "How does capitalism work when consumers have no money?" Then, "Without the workers paying taxes, how does the government function?" And finally, "Without taxes, where does the money for the universal basic income come from?"

All that being said, the true reality of a solution for the AI and robots involves regulating them. Sadly, with Mad Musk having helped to hand the 2024 election to Trump, his reward is near-nonexistent government regulation or oversight. Then, without government protections, and because 'free market' corporations always want efficiencies, AI and robots will probably happen by default.

If you're a young person, you will have seen that I'm, sadly, not too optimistic about law, accounting, management consulting, or banking for careers. However, I'm more of a PEEC person: Playing. Entertaining. Engineering and Creative.

What makes us human, apart from a heart, a brain, and blood pumping through our veins, is that we possess emotions, feelings, and a soul. Neither AI nor a robot has any of these characteristics; thus, all they can ever do is mimic a human, which means everything is about the destination and never the journey. Sadly, this doesn't seem to be an impediment for Hollywood studios, who must be salivating at the prospect of replacing actors, directors, and the thousands of other people who make up a production crew with AI[200].

Those who this new technology may find harder to hurt are people like bestselling author Stephen King. Unlike him, AI will never stay up for hours on end honing its words, developing its characters, and sculpting its plot, all in service of writing the perfect novel.

Nor can a robot ever replace a performer like Taylor Swift, singing in front of a stadium filled with a hundred thousand adoring Swifties.

Those fans came to see her because they are connected to her, and her lyrics and melodies mean something to them.

We can go on. No robot player will take us to the heart and soul of overtime at a Super Bowl. With it all on the line, even with Kansas City Chiefs quarterback Patrick Mahomes' body and mind pushed to the limits of endurance, he keeps on working miracles.

There can only be one Stephen King, Taylor Swift, or Patrick Mahomes. Theirs is the story of human spirit and endeavor. Theirs is also an analog world, where viewers and fans imagine it could be them within the pages of the novel, or on the stage, or on the field. In doing so, they take us to the very essence of our humanity, which no heartless AI or factory-built robot can ever replicate.

But don't just think it's superstars who are invaluable. For the more technical folks, there is engineering. I have a broad definition of this, which includes professions such as construction, carpentry, painting, and plumbing. Also, assuming a Democratic win in 2028, the 'electric' future will need millions of electricians, technicians, and engineers.

Just before we end, by late 2024, some of the hellish future you have read about became a dystopian reality. In Changping, China, Xiaomi, the world's second-largest smartphone manufacturer, opened the world's first 'dark factory.'[201] It's so named because there are no lights. The reason: there are no humans. This 100% robot-operated smartphone factory runs 24/7, 365 days a year, to churn out one phone a second. So dedicated to the cause of efficiency is this corporation that there aren't even any cleaners in the factory, as the machines clean up after themselves.

To conclude, regardless of who you are or what career you choose, my advice for the future is to elect politicians who will regulate AI and robots, perhaps with a 'People Over Robots Act.' It would be very simple. Wherever a robot takes over a worker's job, the company has to keep paying the worker's salary and benefits for ten years. Then watch how quickly these corporations decide robots aren't quite the future that they gaslit us to believe they were.

Chapter 9

How To Make Cops Love Liberals.

I f you're about to switch off, saying policing doesn't interest you, bear your own self-interest in mind by joining the dots to see how connected you really are to the people at the sharp end of policing.

If you're a young man who wants to save American democracy in 2028, then you should know that it is people of color who vote 90% Democratic to preserve democracy. If you're a young woman, furious that Trump and his MAGA freaks stole your right to control what happens to your own body, you should know people of color who vote Democratic were voting to preserve your rights. And, if you're a suburban American parent, terrified someone else's damaged kid may give yours a practical lesson in how an AR-15 works, then people of color are your allies.

I'm thinking of people of color voting in swing states like Michigan, Pennsylvania, and Wisconsin in 2026 and 2028. With their votes, Democrats can take back America to introduce more policies to protect women's rights, strengthen voting rights, slow down global warming, and implement gun control. This is what interest convergence looks like, and if even a small proportion of people of color feel like no one cares, then, as we saw in 2024, we all lose.

If you're like me, you'll never worry about a police car driving behind you, you'll never worry about being pulled over, and you'll never worry that one false move could have a scared cop drawing his weapon on you.

But not all our fellow Americans are so lucky. This is why we need to talk about police reform.

As you read this chapter, it will neither be a puff piece for 'Blue Lives Matter' nor a sledgehammer against 'fascist pigs.' I wanted to approach the issue in a way that might not have been thought of. I promise, whichever side of the issue you fall on, it will be fascinating.

Across America, there are around 473,000 local law enforcement officers[202]. They are spread over 14,700 police departments in fifty states[203]. Two-thirds of officers work in the largest police departments, which are mainly in the metropolitan areas. Think Chicago, Los Angeles, and New York. However, three-quarters of US police departments have less than twenty-five employees.

As far as reforms go, Chuck Wexler, the executive director of the Police Executive Research Forum, said,

> You want to change American policing, figure out how to get to ... the departments of 50 officers or less,"_"How do you reach them? How do you get to them? ... That's what the American people keep wondering.[204]

From the outset, understand that policing will never change until police officers themselves can be persuaded that it is in their own self-interest to change. To do so will need us to make officers our friends. I can hear some of you shouting about police abuse, and at no point will I argue there aren't bad cops. The actual number may be quite small, but, as with crime, it's the perception that matters. Nonetheless, I have to believe that most officers are decent, well-meaning, and want to help, and that the problem is less with individual officers than with the system itself.

As far as that system goes. It's a fact that officers are policing a society where there are over four hundred million guns. It's also a fact that fear-based training at police academies instills in officers the 'warrior' mindset[205]. This leads to them being scared that any of the fifty-three million police/public interactions each year could turn lethal. Matters are not helped by the television news or movies indoctrinating regular citizens to think that a cop's life is all car chases, shoot-outs, and SWAT raids[206].

Before the end of the chapter, we will debunk many myths and see that there are straightforward solutions to fix policing that will help make both citizens' and cops' lives better, but first, we need to get policing in context. For that, we need to talk about drugs and militarized policing. This takes us to Richard Milhous Nixon. In order to win the presidency in 1968, he had to terrify white people. Being a man of exceptionally challenged morality, his chosen path was the demonization of blacks and liberals.

So, in 1971, he manufactured the "War on Drugs." In that case, conservatives used a fear of marijuana and would claim, without evidence, that it was a 'gateway drug' to all manner of unholy endeavors. Obviously coming from Nixon, anti-blackness was at the heart of the 'War.' Don't take my word for it. This is from Nixon's former White House Counsel, John Ehrlichman;

> You want to know what this was really all about?" ...."The Nixon campaign in 1968, and the Nixon White House after that, had two enemies: the anti-war left and black people. You understand what I'm saying? We knew we couldn't make it illegal to be either against the war or black, but by getting the public to associate the hippies with marijuana and blacks with heroin, and then criminalizing both heavily, we could disrupt those communities. We could arrest their leaders, raid their homes, break up their meetings, and vilify them night after night on the evening news. Did we know we were lying about the drugs? Of course, we did.[207]

We can talk about militarized Special Weapons And Tactics, or SWAT teams. These were born after the 1965 Watts protests. Today, they are mostly used to smash down doors, looking for as little as one joint that will allow them to seize a citizen's home[208]. Or I could tell you about the 1033 program, a Department of Defense scheme to funnel excess military-grade weapons to police departments[209]. Started by George H. W. Bush in 1990, it is this that gifts your local police military equipment last used by soldiers in Afghanistan and Iraq. This includes armored personnel carriers, grenade launchers, and even tanks[210].

We could hear about the fear-based training cops undergo that explains something of why they shoot unarmed citizens. That training drums into them to never be a casualty. But here's the paradox of cops looking like the military and acting like the military, all without being trained like the military. When combat units go into battle, they fully expect to take casualties, which is why squads have medics. However, what people may not know is that soldiers' constant training minimizes the chances of taking casualties in the first place.

Perhaps you imagine this method of policing is necessary as violence against police officers is at an insane level. According to the FBI, in 2024, out of 600,000 local and federal law enforcement officers in America, forty-seven were killed in the line of duty[211]. Each death is tragic, but to put matters into perspective, that's 7.8 deaths per 100,000 law-enforcement officers, which is only slightly higher than the average homicide rate amongst American civilians[212].

Militarized policing is also a long way from 'to serve and protect.' Indeed, it sends an appalling message to communities: that this is a war zone, you're the enemy, and we need all this military gear because you are so dangerous.

With these tools in the arsenal, shooting someone at a traffic stop might seem like a restraint of the actual force they could have used.

And when you have a hammer, you'd better believe everything looks like a nail. In 2023, US police killed 1232 citizens. Many were justified. However, in one-third of cases, the suspects were fleeing and posed no threat[213].

This is terrible, but another big problem with militarized policing is who you attract as recruits: young, immature meatheads who want to crack skulls and kick in doors. Unlike Canada, where officers undergo twice the amount of training hours, or England, where it's four times, or Germany, where it's six times[214], in America an eighteen-year-old can, after just four months of training, walk the streets with a badge and a gun and, thanks to qualified immunity[215]—the arcane legal construct that requires a plaintiff to either cite an identical legal precedent or rely on the testimony from other officers before they can claim damages—the power to do almost anything they want to a citizen.

For those citizens who do overcome the qualified immunity hurdle, you may have heard about the multi-million-dollar civil suit settlements for wrongful deaths. What you may not know is that these never come out of the police budget[216]. After George Floyd was murdered, the taxpayers of the City of Minneapolis paid out $27 million to George Floyd's family. Just to put that figure into context, it's nearly the same as the $28 million that the city allocates to healthcare spending for its four hundred thou-sand residents for a whole year. So, when you hear the far-right BS about 'crumbling inner cities,' remember that those millions of dollars in payouts all mean less funding for roads, hospitals, and schools.

Citizens being shot is tragic, but it's not the norm. Being preyed on, however, is. It's called 'predatory policing[217].' This may be the most perni-cious aspect of modern policing that few people know about. Yet, for folks in urban areas, it's a reality of life.

An oft-quoted GOP lie is that cops stop black motorists because that's where the crime is. Bear in mind that traffic stops make up nearly twenty million out of the fifty-three million police interactions with the public each year[218]. It's here where the powerful get to prey upon the powerless.

Forget duffel bags full of marijuana or machine guns. The traffic stop is a great excuse for a shakedown. A lot of what we learn is predatory policing stems from inequality. The poorer the driver, the more likely a cop can find something wrong with their car. A suburban dad's three-year-old BMW is probably not going to have anything wrong with it, whereas the inner-city man's twenty-year-old Toyota Camry might well do.

It was once said the poor are not just poor in money; they're poor in the choices they make. I would add that being poor is a full-time job, as it's goddamn stressful having no money. Just going back to that man's Toyota Camry. What if it's a choice between fixing his muffler or putting gas in his car so that he can get to work to earn the money to pay to fix the muffler?

So it is that a traffic stop that would just be an inconvenience for me or a soccer mom may be a life-altering event for low-income folks. This is not my imagination. In 2015, following the police killing of an unarmed black man, Michael Brown in Ferguson, Missouri, and the subsequent public uprising and birth of the Black Lives Matter movement[219], the Department of Justice issued two reports. The first, which garnered the most attention, was on the unlawful nature of the killing. However, the second was arguably even more important: a 102-page report detailing how the Ferguson Police Department was a tax collection arm of the local government[220]. Indeed, to this day, fines and fees are Ferguson's second-largest source of revenue[221].

It works like this. Officers were tasked with raising as much money as they could from the local inner-city population. In practice, this meant one traffic stop might result in eight separate citations, amounting to perhaps $1,000 in fines. Unfortunately, the low-income citizen who can't pay the fines would be summoned to court. As non-payment of these fines is a criminal offense, if they don't pay, they get a criminal record and possibly jail time. All this punishment simply ensures they can never get a decent job to earn any money to have a decent life, and so the vicious wheel of poverty spins.

Just to be sure that Ferguson wasn't an isolated red state problem, we can see what Rosa Brooks, a law professor at Georgetown University Law Center who became a police officer in Washington, D.C., and wrote about her experiences in 2021's 'Tangled Up in Blue: Policing the American City,' said:

> In the business of revenue raising, if the Police department wanted to, they could nearly bankrupt a citizen with fines. We were authorized to conduct traffic stops and issue tickets for people driving too fast; driving too slowly; driving with improperly affixed, illegible, or improperly illuminated tags; driving with the front, rear, side, or windshield obstructed; or driving with a sign or other unauthorized item attached to the mirror, window, or window frame. The pamphlet listing moving violations and parking violations ran to thirteen pages.[222]

Just imagine another world where the police department of Sarasota, Florida, introduced a new policy. They plotted their officers in patrol cars near a local school, then started pulling over soccer moms for the infractions you just read about. And every offense meant an extra $100 fine. Think how quickly the police would lose the trust of the suburbs.

So now you've had a grounding in modern, mostly urban policing, what do you think about the slogan 'Defund the Police'?

Back in 2020, the people shouting that knew everything you've just read. It was the lazy corporate media who misreported it as abolishing policing, which terrified many people. However, at the heart of defunding is asking whether we actually need police acting as social workers.

To help to answer this, we can look to research drawn by organizations like the Vera Institute of Justice. They have conducted extensive research detailing what cops do.

Between 2019 and 2021, they analyzed 911 'calls for service' from nine cities, including Baltimore, Detroit, New Orleans, and Seattle. Out of nearly sixteen million calls, two-thirds were non-criminal, requiring no arrest; incidents such as "fireworks, abandoned cars, or pets on the loose." Another one-fifth of calls were mental health cases that also didn't need police intervention. Less than three in one hundred cases involved violent crime[223].

The New York Times backed this up. They reported that, based on the 911 calls in New Orleans, Montgomery, Maryland, and Sacramento, less than 4% of calls for service involved violence[224].

Knowing that many people need help rather than handcuffs, we can look to the brilliant CAHOOTS: Crisis Assistance Helping Out On The Streets[225]. This ingenious program has been running successfully in Eugene, Oregon, since 1989. A crisis counselor and an EMT take on some of the tasks that police were never trained for, like domestic arguments, mental health calls, and medical emergencies.

For just 2% of the police budget, CAHOOTS answers one in every six police calls for service. CAHOOTS cannot predict how a mentally unstable person may act, yet despite this, studies have shown that they only need to call in police assistance in 1% of cases.

Consider this. Does a cop really need to attend a domestic dispute? Or move an unhoused person out of a park? Or take a truant child back to school? Or deal with drug addicts? Imagine if you saw a mentally disturbed person in a shopping center. Who do you reckon could better deal with them, a trained counselor or an armed police officer? People in crisis need help, not a police cell.

It's also worth mentioning that a quarter of all officer-involved killings are of mentally disturbed people[226]. These result in those multi-million-dollar lawsuits that impact the city budget. So, even if local politicians don't give a damn about the mentally ill, they do care about the city budget. Thus, fewer lawsuits mean lower taxes and better re-election prospects.

In New York, there is a similar program being run on a small scale, operating out of Fire Station 55 in Harlem and the Bronx, called 'B-HEARD': The Behavioral Health Emergency Assistance Response Division. If a 911 call comes in involving a mental health crisis and there is no indication of the threat of violence, an unarmed EMT and social worker are dispatched.

In 2022, over the first six months of the program, New York City said that 911 operators had diverted nearly a quarter of mental health calls in the few precincts where the program was in place.

These programs highlight one of the greatest problems for cops: officers always have to keep moving, so they only have two choices: arrest or ambulance. By contrast, an EMT and social worker team like B-HEARD can take their time, even up to an hour[227].

To give some idea of how many mentally ill people cops come into contact with, up to half the nearly two million people in US prisons have mental conditions[228]. In fact, today, prisons are, by default, the largest mental facilities in America. Now, can you imagine a worse place to put a mentally vulnerable person than a prison?

Once again, to my imaginary conservative readers, even if you don't care about mentally ill people, perhaps you do care about the cost of incarceration. In West Virginia, it costs $46,000 per year. In Wisconsin, $66,000. If you head down south to Florida, Louisiana, or Texas, where Republicans place little value on human life, people can be locked up for under $30,000, but still, those are your taxes being wasted on punishment instead of treatment[229].

At this point, we need to look at the reason for the abhorrent situation. As ever, it comes down to money. With approximately 1.8 million Americans locked up, at an average cost of $45,000 a year, that's an $80 billion prison-industrial complex[230]. This means a lot of federal agents, cops, lawyers, judges, prison, and probation staff all earning a living. As they are spread across the 435 congressional districts and 3143 counties, it's also 80 billion stubborn reasons fighting against the system ever changing.

Which brings us to another huge reason why most police reforms die: the solid concrete barrier of recalcitrance that is the police union. Just to quickly segue, these unions are the polar opposite of any other trade union, which works to make members' working conditions and lives better. By contrast, Trump-supporting police unions only believe in harsh measures and resist anything that reduces the police budget or puts restraints on the use of force.

To get an idea of what sort of characters we are talking about, let's cast our gaze over the January 6th insurrection, in which Trump terrorists beat and murdered Capitol police officers. Few may know that in the aftermath, four officers committed suicide. Bearing in mind what had just happened to his brothers in blue, John Catanzara, head of the Chicago police union, one of the nation's largest, offered this;

> If the worst crime here is trespassing, so be it. But to call these people treasonous is beyond ridiculous and ignorant.[231].

Then we have the International Union of Police Associations, which offered not one ounce of criticism of Trump. Quite the contrary. In 2024, they would say, "President Trump's history of support for the men and women of law enforcement is unmatched."[232]

As these police unions always say NO to any form of reform, perhaps it's time to force them to look at their members' lives. Harsh policing isn't just traumatic for citizens; it's terrible for cops too. They are under assault, under threat, and in danger—from their own minds! Divorce rates and alcohol abuse are all higher in officers' lives[233]. But it gets worse. According to the DOJ, one in five officers suffers from PTSD[234]. This might partly explain why cops are 54% more likely to commit suicide than civilians[235].

Knowing all this, it's criminal that these fat cat bosses do nothing, even though they know officers are being sent out onto the streets, day in and day out, to see some of the worst that citizens do to each other, but also that society does to its own citizens. Oh and, if the harsh, 'tough-guy' method of policing actually worked, America wouldn't be the high-income world's most violent society, with its highest prison population[236].

All this being said, there are police departments acting as pathfinders to show how to make everyone's lives better. Alexandria, Kentucky, is a town of 10,000 people. Against initial resistance, the police department employed two social workers in their under twenty-officer department.

One case that prompted this was a Vietnam veteran who was suffering from PTSD. He called 911 over sixty times in one year. Each time, cops would have to show up and calm him down. Nothing they did had any effect. However, once the social workers came on the scene, they were able to get him treated through the Veterans Administration[237]. This is again where the "Defund" comes in; some of the police budget needs to be sent to pay for these workers.

As far as policies go, nothing can happen until after a Democratic victory in 2028. At that time, if we want to reform policing, this is where we start. We have seen that self-interest is the key to effecting change, so it is that before we get to ending the 'War on Drugs,' predatory policing, or qualified immunity, we have to win over a proportion of those 600,000 officers.

To start, we need to show officers how their lives can be better. My tagline is 'Less Work. Less Stress. Same Pay."

That's got half of them interested straight away. After all, who wouldn't want that? We could start in those 12,000 departments (making up 3/4 of US PDs) with less than twenty-five employees. It's here where change can be implemented most quickly, simply because there is less inertia. As for those Trump-loving police unions. Now they will be put on the back foot by being forced to argue against their members having better lives.

Democrats could, through the federal government, offer one million dollars per department towards the cost of three EMTs and three social workers to deal with calls related to 'social work' issues, like homelessness, addiction, and mental health. The cost would be just $12.2 billion.

Even if just a quarter of these small departments took up the offer, their officers would feel the weight being taken off their shoulders and their lives getting better. Then word will spread to the other more reticent areas as well as larger urban departments, and they will want it too. We can call the program "HELP COPS, HELP US."

Now, with cops as our friends, all the other reforms can start. Many cleverer folks have written about this, but one of the first must be to end predatory policing; if politicians want to raise taxes, let them send out their own tax collectors.

Then, with all the other reforms that are now possible, perhaps one day, we might even see cops patrolling the South side of Chicago on bicycles.

Chapter 10

When Crime Was Just Another Path To a Beautiful Home.

The TV series Fargo is a sublime epic. Its creator and writer, Noah Hawley, is not just a masterful storyteller, he's also a phenomenal observer of America. There are many remarkable scenes, but one sticks in my mind from season four. It takes place in Kansas City, Missouri, in the 1950s. In the scene, an Italian-American crime boss is explaining to his rival African-American gang members the reality of America;

> You know why America loves a crime story? Because America is a crime story. But here's the rub. When we hear a crime story, who do we root for? Not the poor sap that got taken, the victim. No. We root for the taker, the guy with the gat. See, this country loves a man, who takes what he wants. Unless that man looks like you. Capisce? See, Johnny Society looks at me, they see a fella that's using crime to get ahead. But you? All they see is crime. And that's why you're going to lose. Cause I can take all the money and pussy I want, and still run for President. But you? It's always going to be the rope.[238]

Back in the 1950s, leather-jacket-wearing Arthur Fonzerelli—The Fonz, from the hit 1970s television show, Happy Days—would have been considered quite 'ethnic,' and, being Catholic, still treated with suspicion by White Anglo Sason Protestant (WASP) America[239]. However, to get ahead, folks like The Fonz received a little 'help.'

In those days, every ethnic community in a city had their own crime, and we have the stories to prove it. Italians were featured in Mean Streets and The Godfather[240]. The Irish are represented with Gangs of New York and The Departed, and the Jewish with Once Upon a Time in America.

It's instructive to remember that the evolution of these ethnic criminal areas was before heroin and cocaine, so the mainstay of their income would have been from extortion, hijacking, liquor, and prostitution, and when the drugs came, they were all pumped into black communities.

Ethnic gangs were tolerated by both the authorities and their own communities because of a concept known as the 'Defended Neighborhood.'[241] These gangs kept a semblance of order on the streets, and that order meant the vast majority of ordinary, law-abiding people could go about their business. Of course, extortion was a price the community paid for this stability.

However, essentially, ethnic-white gang crime allowed for communities to flourish by bringing opportunity to their neighborhoods. This meant an on-ramp to the American Dream for some Irish, Italian, and Jewish Americans.

Thanks, in part to the seeds the criminals had planted, the communities could field a crop of their own councilmen and congressmen, and build a power structure that would fight for them.

So it would be that, within just two generations, if you have the name Gambino, Giancana, or Gotti, you are more likely to be a doctor, lawyer, or real estate developer than anything to do with the Mafia.

Which brings us to the 'inner cities.' Here was where those white gangs pumped in the drugs and the police smashed down on the crime, and so opportunity never got a chance to show its face.

Even if modern criminals could, it's too late for them to offer their version of the 'defended neighborhood'. So, as the gangs don't have any ability to attain political power or legitimate influence, they have no stake; thus, they stay involved in crime. And without a power structure to fight for local citizens, progress is very glacial.

Just on the point of crime. The facts, courtesy of the FBI, are that violent crime has been on a massive downward trend since the 1990s. The only upturn was during COVID, when the whole world experienced an increase[242].

Sadly, the news will not report this. Combine that with so much 'reality' TV, true crime podcasts, and fictional TV shows about crime, and suddenly, fantasy and reality weave themselves together, leading to the perception that crime is everywhere. Of course, 'crime' doesn't mean Wall Street.

So it is today that politicians and the media love to report on the slightest black infraction. This isn't anecdotal. A 2010 study for the National Institute of Health revealed that black crime was twice as likely to be reported on as white crime[243].

From all those stories, people can feel scared should they see three young men coming towards them in hoodies. That feeling of being scared or uncomfortable is personal, and it's painful, and we want it to go away. So, out of stage left, strolls 'law and order,' whether Democrat or Republican, promising to clean up the streets. And if along the way, a couple of black men should get shot by cops, well...

But here's the truth. I lived in London in the 1990s. It was a city of eight million people, and I've never been assaulted, burgled, carjacked, robbed, stabbed, or shot; and, whatever the opposite of a sheltered life is—I've led it.

All peer-reviewed studies show that, in cities, serious crime is concentrated in certain blocks[244]. Most city-dwellers live far away from any drugs and shootings, and even if they do live on the less salubrious side of town, the chances of any middle-class person being violently assaulted or murdered are vanishingly slim. How do I know? Because if it happened, it would be headline news...for a month.

This gets us to one of the fastest ways to get rid of crime and raise the standard of living in inner cities. Just make neighborhoods pretty. The prettier the neighborhood, the higher the property values and the lower the crime.

There's a reason drug dealers don't peddle their poison on Manhattan's Upper East Side. It's also why kids aren't using nine-millimeter pistols to settle scores on suburban streets. People with nice homes don't want criminals outside screwing with their property values.

Here, though, is where we reach a brutal truth that 'color-blind' liberals will never talk about. It goes back to that concept of the 'defended neighborhood.' Whether it is Baltimore, Detroit, Memphis, or New York, black political muscle is insufficient to get investors to plow money into a new black neighborhood. For receipts, I offer you fifty years of crumbling inner cities.

There are much better books about why this is. However, essentially, from the 1950s onwards, white flight to the suburbs took with it the businesses and the employment and gutted the city tax base[245].

So it is, the fastest way to build black wealth in any inner city is through urban regeneration or 'gentrification.' In the past, this meant 'relocating' local residents. Of course, that ensured that they never got to share in the wealth, but it doesn't have to be this way.

As self-interest is the essence of motivating people, we need to gather a coalition of both existing residents, together with incoming (young) white, black, and brown folks. This is the key that unlocks the door to beautiful new homes in a clean, safe community that people can be proud of living in. You may be wondering how to fit all these residents in; well, it's a city, so just build up, for the sky is the limit. As far as funding goes, federal or municipal bonds, rather than Wall Street vultures, could be used.

With these new communities, people will see that when wealth comes to town, drug dealers and criminals find themselves out of business; after all, without desperation and poverty, poisonous sedation against the pain of life is unnecessary.

But, we're not finished. According to the census bureau, eight out of ten Americans live in urban areas[246]. Here's where more self-interest comes in. With the new vibrant communities, businesses will flock back as they're coming to places with millions of high-spending customers and thousands of workers to serve those customers.

And all that brings taxes back to the city to allow for more development and improvements. That's what a positive feedback loop looks like.

Chapter 11

If You Hate 'Illegals', We Need To Talk About the Southern Border.

Before we start, just know that I believe in both borders and controls on immigration, while fully supporting allowing the best, the brightest, and the most useful workers into America. From those foundations, we are going to have an honest conversation about immigration, the likes of which will make your head spin.

All the way back in 1980, that well-known RINO, Ronald Reagan, said of immigration from the southern border,

> Rather than talking about putting up a fence, why don't we work out some recognition of our mutual problems, make it possible for them to come here legally with a work permit,"_"And then while they're working and earning here,

they pay taxes here. And when they want to go back they can
go back.[247]

In 1984, speaking about undocumented migrants, Reagan opined,

I believe in the idea of amnesty for those who have put down
roots and who have lived here, even though some time back,
they may have entered illegally.[248]

The Gipper lived true to his word when he signed the Immigration Reform and Control Act of 1986. This allowed for undocumented migrants, who were in the country before 1982, to apply for legal status. There were some provisos, such as paying any back taxes and fines and that the migrant learn to speak English and be of 'good moral character.'

Another section of the Act details fines and penalties for businesses that employed undocumented people. They would be exempt if they could prove they had been presented with relatively convincing fake documents. Bear this in mind, as we will come back to it[249].

Since that time, the issue has become hot politically, especially as the eleven million undocumented migrants currently living and working in America are brown and black folks.

This being said, there were possibilities for immigration reform up to 2012. Recall, this was an age before Trump and before social media.

Here we have Sean Hannity of Fox News, for once, getting it right. He was reported in Politico speaking about the immigration reform of 2012 that the Obama administration was attempting to get bipartisan support for;

It's simple to me to fix it," Hannity says. "I think you control
the border first. You create a pathway for those people that

are here — you don't say you've got to go home. And that is a position that I've evolved on. Because, you know what, it's got to be resolved. The majority of people here, if some people have criminal records you can send them home, but if people are here, law-abiding, participating for years, their kids are born here, you know, first secure the border, pathway to citizenship, done.[250]

Unfortunately, the timing of this common-sense thinking was such that it would crash headlong into the precursors of the Confederate Taliban, the Tea Party. These primary-voting, pre-Trump Republicans only had eyes for culture war issues, and they killed any hope of bipartisan legislation.

While, in this chapter, we are talking about 'illegal' immigration, with the rise in the percentage of legal brown and black American citizens, the Confederate Taliban doesn't see much distinction. Thus, in 2024, Trump supporters speak of deporting JD Vance's brown, American wife because she is of Indian origin[251]. Indeed, Trump himself spoke of "shithole countries," echoing the basest nativist sentiments of his angry voters[252].

I lay a lot of blame for the toxicity of the debate at the feet of liberals. For scared Democrats, immigration has traditionally been a third rail issue, with them being terrified to talk to voters about the topic for fear of appearing "soft." Then, in reverse wish fulfillment, their silence confirms their softness, and into the void steps the GOP, more than happy to propagate denigrating and dehumanizing lies about immigrants, whether "crime," "replacement," "stolen jobs," or "welfare cheats."

The latter two are quite puzzling, as how can immigrants be stealing all the jobs and be too lazy to work? But, of course, there's no room for logic in the house of depravity.

I know the right-wing anti-immigration freaks who profess their 'Christianity' have never read the Bible. But imagine what it would do to them if any Democrat, speaking about the Christian refugees at the southern border, actually quoted Jesus' words;

> You shall treat the stranger who sojourns with you as the native among you, and you shall love him as yourself, for you were strangers in the land of Egypt: I am the Lord your God.[253]

Perhaps we should ask why a lot of these folks are making the treacherous journey north. Most of the media coverage focuses on the 'illegal' crossings and the physical border, which is why nothing ever changes. To learn half of the real story of undocumented migration, we need to go back to 1989. That year, President George H. W. Bush announced an expansion of the "War on Drugs," calling it "the greatest domestic threat facing our nation today."[254]

Then, just one year later, in 1990, to control immigration, the US Border Patrol would erect the first-ever border fencing with Mexico, starting with a fourteen-mile stretch in San Diego[255].

It's impossible to separate the migrants at the border and the 'war on drugs.' We know that the war was one of Nixon's many lies. What isn't a lie, though, is the sheer American demand for cocaine, fentanyl, heroin, and marijuana.

Then, the vast amount of money flowing back into the illegal drug trade allows the violent cartels to pay off corrupt cops, prosecutors, judges, and politicians across Latin America. Which leads to more violence and destabilization and more people fleeing.

The simple solution to drugs is to decriminalize, regulate, and tax; suddenly, the supply stops and the Latin American nations stabilize.

The problem is, in America itself, the war on drugs, as we read about in chapter nine, has financed a multi-billion-dollar annual employment industry for cops, federal agents, lawyers, judges and prisons. Thus, if you're a federal agency or a police department making money off this, why would you have any interest or incentive in stopping it and being out of work?

Nonetheless, the fact remains: many of the desperate souls who arrive at the southern border are fleeing drug-related violence, most of it from guns.

This being so, you may have watched TV shows like Narcos or El Chapo and consider Mexico to be corrupt and violent. I can't dispute this. The nation of 127 million people has a gun violence rate 70% higher than in America, with guns being used in two out of every three homicides.

One may assume they must have terribly lax gun laws, but not so fast. Here is a nugget of informational gold from the Los Angeles Times;

> The only gun shop in all of Mexico is behind a fortress-like wall on a heavily guarded military base. To enter the Directorate of Arms and Munitions Sales, customers must undergo months of background checks — six documents are required — and then be frisked by uniformed soldiers." Mexico's Constitution guarantees citizens the right to bear arms. However, "it also stipulates that federal law "will determine the cases, conditions, requirements and places" of gun ownership.

In practice, this means showing, among other items, your birth certificate, proof of employment, and having no criminal record[256].

Something isn't adding up here. If Mexican citizens can't get guns, why is there so much gun violence? In her brilliant 2024 book, "Exit Wounds: How America's Guns Fuel Violence Across The Border," legal and medical anthropologist Ieva Jusionyte sheds light on an astonishing fact that might change the way you think about 'the border' and our southern neighbors;

> One of the major sources of these guns in Mexico are specifically states that have very, very lax gun regulations. Texas is the primary one. Between 2017 and 2021, 43% of all guns recovered in crime scenes in Mexico came from Texas alone. The other 17% come from Arizona, and 13% from California.[257]

That's three states sending at least three-quarters of all guns involved in Mexican crime. The ATF backed this up, offering that 70% of guns recovered in Mexican murders were US-sourced. My head spins, knowing there were more Mexicans in Mexico murdered with American guns than Americans in America murdered with American guns[258].

The ATF estimates approximately 250,000 US guns are smuggled into Mexico each year. These are weapons being used by the cartels to enforce the violence that protects their industries of death. The guns are made by Colt, Smith & Wesson, Ruger, and other US manufacturers, who, thanks to George H.W.'s son, cannot be sued[259].

It's also American guns that are ending up in failed states like Haiti. According to the ATF, nearly nine out of ten of the guns used in violence over there came from America[260].

Back at the southern border, there's a tragically perverse irony in imagining the journey of a truckload of those American guns heading to Mexico to wreak mayhem and violence at exactly the same time as a group of migrants arrive at the border—fleeing the mayhem and violence American guns cause.

Just to that point. Imagine what it takes to leave the land you love. If that's too much, just think about the journey of walking seventy-five miles across the blazing hot Mexican Sonoran Desert.

Then, when you reach America, you're in a strange place, with strange food, strange streets, and strange people. It's a place where you're starting from nothing; your qualifications mean nothing, and you have no connections and no money.

This brings us on to the second part of the story and something else that tepid liberals won't talk about. It was the fantastic John Fugelsang who first put into my head the thought that at the southern border, there is a huge unwritten sign saying, "HELP WANTED."[261] So it is that the vast majority of people crossing the border will do the jobs that Americans don't want to do. For many of the undocumented, there's the field or the meat processing plant. For others, it's the back of the restaurant or cleaning the hotel.

Perhaps you don't know, but it's the undocumented folks who are helping to keep inflation down[262]. They are the ones picking and processing the produce and working in almost every restaurant and hotel in America. By doing so, they ensure you don't have to pay $20 for a salad and $30 for a burger. Yet, for their troubles, the undocumented will receive less than the minimum wage and no worker protections.

Oh, and precisely because coming into contact with the law is to risk deportation, they're very law-abiding but also completely vulnerable to being victims of crime.

Speaking of crime, when Immigration and Customs Enforcement (ICE) raids a meatpacking plant and detains twenty workers, what they never do, thanks to Ronald's 1986 get-out, is go to the back room and arrest, or even fine, the rich bosses employing the undocumented folk.

For a receipt, we just need to visit America's most persistent criminal. Whether at Trump Tower in the 1980s, his Bedminster Golf Course in New Jersey, or his poor man's Xanadu in Florida, the felon employed hundreds of undocumented workers, without consequence[263].

It was the extraordinary Texas liberal columnist, Molly Ivins, who wrote in 2006;

Should you actually want to stop Mexicans and OTMs (other than Mexicans) from coming to the United States, here is how to do it: Find an illegal worker at a large corporation. This is not difficult; brooms and mops are big tip-offs. Then put the CEO of that corporation in prison for two or more years for violating the law against hiring illegal workers. Got it?. and, just to make sure, put some Betty Sue Billups housewife, preferably one with blonde hair in a flip in the joint for a two-year stretch for hiring a Mexican gardener. When there are no jobs for illegal workers, they do not come. Got it?[264]

This far into the book, you're probably an expert at recognizing insincerity and hypocrisy, so recall that the same bosses of the businesses that exploit cheap, undocumented labor then use the profits from that labor to fund the GOP politicians who blame Democrats for the "crisis" at the border.

This takes us to the exact point of how Democrats screw up. After three years of BS fear-mongering about the border by the media and the GOP, the Biden Administration tried to enact one of the harshest bipartisan immigration reforms of the modern age. It was basically a GOP wish list, ably assisted by 'moderate' Democrats. Trump killed it because smashing down on brown and black people is all he has to run on[265].

As ever, meek, weak Democrats wouldn't even pick the lowest-hanging fruit. All they had to do was to tell voters that, for two whole years from 2016 to 2018, Trump and the GOP held the presidency, the House, and Senate, and had a 5-4 majority on the Supreme Court. From that, everything and anything was possible, yet the GOP did nothing.

Ironically, my receipt comes from someone who picked that fruit, Republican Rep. Chip Roy of Texas. He offered this in 2024;

We're not going to just pass the buck and say any president can just walk in and secure the border." "I saw former president Trump make that allegation earlier today on one of his social media posts. All a president has to do is declare the border is closed, and it's closed. Well, with all due respect, that didn't happen in 2017, 2018, 2019, and 2020.[266]

Don't imagine that Mr. Roy is any friend of migrants. Indeed, in his public statements, he speaks of them invading the US and coming to trash America[267]. As a 'true believer' though, he wants the border closed, and this bill was one way to reach that goal. That's why he was so pissed to find out that Trump really didn't care.

Clearly, I'm not troubled by internecine struggles within the Republican Party. Instead, my most damning indictments are aimed at Democrats. After all, everything you have read in this chapter is easy to find.

For any of the hundreds of Democrats in Congress or the Administration, the campaign ads on fake Christians, gun smuggling, and inflation-busting workers almost write themselves. Yet, in the 2024 campaign, not one Democrat had the common sense to use any of this as fighting talk to smash the GOP with.

Chapter 12

Meeting The Mythical Man In The Mid-West Diner

Academics have poured over the data as to who brought Trump to power in 2016 and garnered him even more votes in 2020 and 2024. What were the driving forces behind this phenomenon? Was it America's shifting demographics? Was it fueled by racism? Was it due to economic anxiety? Or perhaps it was the desire of people to disrupt the system? Research from Stanford, MIT, and Oxford University found one simple predictor of Trump support in 2016: unhappiness.

They drew from over two million surveys and, in their words;

> Unhappiness predicted the Trump vote better than race, income levels, or unemployment, how many immigrants had moved into the county, or how old or religious the citizens were. And it did so among both whites and non-whites alike. Unhappiness also predicted the Trump election better than other subjective variables, like how people thought the economy was going or would be going in the future.[268]

In my book, The Confederate Taliban, I describe the SCARI five strands of Republican voters: the Scared, (fake) Christian, The Angry, the Rich and the Insane.

It's important to note that the 'unhappiness' that drives the votes of most Republican voters has to do with the changing nature of American society. In the latter four guises, the Confederate Taliban is furious at challenges to the patriarchy, proposals to tax the rich, or having to hear about, or from, previously marginalized people. We know that most of these people are unrecoverable.

However, you may have heard the phrase 'show compassion for the conned and contempt for the con men.' I'm thinking of the 10% of 2016 Obama/Trump voters. These were people who felt that they weren't getting a fair deal and wanted someone to fight for them. Apart from the non-voters, these are the only potentially winnable GOP voters.

As these folks will not make the first move, it's crucial to meet them where they are. They may be quite straight-talking and patriotic and may have slightly unreconstructed views (as much from lack of contact as anything else) still on race and equal rights. But like everyone else in America, they are primarily driven by the self-interest of what's best for them and their family.

This being so, let's take an imaginary trip back to 2015 and meet Dave Burnett, a fifth-generation Pennsylvanian living in Westmoreland County. His family immigrated from Scotland in the 1800s and settled in the Appalachian Mountains. Then, during the Great Depression, they migrated to southwestern Pennsylvania in search of work.

Dave is a non-college educated 45-year-old, who is married with a teenage son and daughter. He works as a Line Supervisor at a national electrical cable manufacturer in Pittsburgh and earns $50,000 a year. His wife, Jenny, works in the administration department at a local hospital and earns $27,000 a year. Their $77,000 household income puts them right in the middle of the middle-class[269]. However, after paying their taxes, mortgage, health insurance, college fund, car payments, fuel, gas, electricity, food, and household bills, they have no money left over for savings at the end of the month.

Dave is the kind of guy the New York Times is after when they hit up those Midwestern diners, in search of the elusive 'swing voter.' He voted for Obama in 2008 but Romney in 2012. He'd identify as Christian but doesn't attend church. He loves deer hunting with his buddies but doesn't open-carry. There are a few black folks at his workplace, but he doesn't know any of them outside of work. The same goes for Asian, Latino, or LGBTQ+ people. It's not because he is prejudiced; it's just that he knows the people he grew up with in the town he grew up in, and he's never really considered it any differently.

One day, Dave goes to work and gets hit with the news that his factory is moving to Mexico. The company blamed costs, but let's be real, they just wanted the low wages, low regulations, and low taxes, all to boost their profits.

Regardless of their reasons, now Dave's got no job, no healthcare, and is facing the grim prospect of losing his home. For a forty-five-year-old man with a family to support and bills to pay, it's a tough spot to be in.

People lucky enough to have savings or investments have the comfort of "mental bandwidth."[270] Through the luxury of that financial cushion, should economic misfortune strike, they don't face the anxiety of their home or car being repossessed. For those this fortunate, bad fortune never hits them so hard.

For those not so lucky, the stress of not knowing how they're going to get through a financial event is like physical pain, with the 'Devil's Cocktail' of cortisol and adrenaline surging through their bodies[271]. Most of us have experienced a stress-related tension headache, which usually passes after sleep, but what if the cause of the stress doesn't go away?

So, here's Dave, at home searching for a decent-paying job that will feed his family. He wants to work, and he's capable of working. The lessons that he's grown up with were that a man should be strong and independent. But now, when he's vulnerable, he's hearing all this talk of "white privilege" and "Black Lives Matter."

From there it's easy to fall into the toxic trifecta of Fox News, far-right podcasters, AM radio, and the GOP. They will feed a seductive yet spurious narrative: *"latte-sipping, EV-driving, America-hating, weak-ass liberals have allowed Mexicans to steal our jobs....and work-shy blacks to get all the welfare.... all whilst hard-working 'real' Americans are getting screwed over and discriminated against."*

From that message of fear and outrage, his eyes are finally open to the 'real' cause of his problems, and now he sees an enemy to focus on: the changing America, and he doesn't like what he sees. He's not physically scared, just scared of what his future place in America will look like, and that fear will always find comfort in fury, for fury offers the simple remedy of erasing the cause of the fear.

From a cognitive perspective, it's understandable. He constantly hears that people of color, new immigrants, women, and LGBTQ folks will make his life worse. Then, as his life is deteriorating, he notices an increase in the representation of those groups, and it can feel like the prophecy is coming true.

Social scientists can explain to Dave about correlation and causation, or how immigrants commit less crime than native-born citizens while still contributing taxes[272]. They can talk about confirmation bias and motivated reasoning—how we only seek information that supports our beliefs and dismiss any information that contradicts them, even when it is true[273]. Economists can then shed light on how automation and offshoring by greedy corporations are responsible for the majority of the decline in jobs[274].

However, when people are under stress, they don't think rationally, and their minds take shortcuts to find the simplest explanation[275]. Factor in many people's inability to think critically and a bias to trust those we like, even when they deceive us. Then mix in that self-interest is the greatest motivator in deciding who to vote for, and watch them cast their ballot for a candidate who lies that things can go right back to the boom days of the 1950s, when people like them were on top.

Lyndon Johnson grew up as a dirt-poor, working-class outsider from the South[276]. Perhaps his personal experience of rich people screwing over working people combined with his towering character allowed him to be a much better man than society needed him to be[277]. Way back in the 1960s, he saw through the Confederate Taliban's game. He shared his insight with his staffer, Bill Moyers:

> If you can convince the lowest white man he's better than the best-colored man, he won't notice you're picking his pocket. Hell, give him somebody to look down on, and he'll empty his pockets for you.[278]

Pretty much since LBJ, Democrats have been 'race silent,' because they are so scared of upsetting the apple cart. Into that void, oozes the GOP with the right-wing 'dog whistle.' I understand that in 2024, the whistle has been replaced with a bullhorn, but the principal remains.

Their code words for white are 'Hardworking,' 'Christian,' or 'Suburban' (never mind that most black folks live in the suburbs too). They also use terms like "inner city" and "crime" when referring to black communities. These can be very persuasive, as our brains are wired to respond to fear above all else, and in the changing America, fear is a very easy condition to catch, and not just for white folks.

To this point, in the 2024 election, while Trump's vote share among white voters stood at 57%—within a point or two of every GOP candidate since George W. Bush—he saw gains with male Latino, Asian, and, to a lesser extent, black voters[279]. This was illustrated by the shift in votes in big urban cities like New York, Miami-Dade, Los Angeles, Cook County (Chicago), and Wayne County (Detroit)[280].

Part of the explanation for this was the endless lies about 'illegals' and 'crime' and tactics like the Republican ploy of 'busing' undocumented folks to the big cities. Add in the poisonous disinformation spread on social media platforms of migrants receiving cash and free homes[281]. Then, factor in that there was hardly any pushback against the GOP lies from the corporate media or Democrats.

Now put yourself in the shoes of some of these voters, worried that the migrants' skill set might place them in direct competition for employment, and see how easy it would be to fall into the right-wing trap.

For others, again, it's self-interest. These black and brown voters may not know that when Trump supporters speak of 'mass deportations,' they don't distinguish between a Palestinian, a Pakistani, or a Puerto Rican. However, they understand that more anger towards newly arrived people of color means more anger towards them, so they short-sightedly vote for the party that will stop the other people of color from coming in.

None of this is new. It's the simple divide-and-conquer tactic that Democrats, despite having all the information from the last chapter, are terrified of combating. So, as nature abhors a vacuum, voters moved to the candidate who promised a 'solution.'

You may know the expression "you can catch more flies with honey than with vinegar." The basic fact is that in order to sell something to someone, you need to get them to trust you. But, in order to get them to trust you, first you need to get them to like you. This is why all successful salespeople smile a lot and are friendly.

As far as a winning messaging strategy goes, it exists today as the Race/Class Narrative (RCN)[282]. It was created jointly by Ian Haney Lopez, professor of public law at UC Berkeley School of Law; Heather McGhee, former president of the think tank, Demos and the author of The Sum of Us, and political strategist and messaging supremo Anat Shenker-Osorio.

In his groundbreaking book, 'Merge Left, Fusing Race and Class, Winning Elections, and Saving America,' Professor Haney Lopez describes the three sides of the left. We have seen the moderate 'race-silent' types. Then there's the 'class left,' who say, forget race, it's class that matters. Unfortunately, their messaging isn't potent enough to beat the dog-whistle racist message. The third style of left-wing messaging is the "race left," for whom everything is about race first. Unfortunately, this one simply scares the pants off many white people.

But, never fear, to defang far-right messaging, all Democrats have to do is talk about race, but link it to class.

In Anat Shenker-Osorio, we have a genius messenger who shows the key to this messaging. Using a crushingly effective three-part strategy, she gives us a surefire way to defang the right-wing dog-whistle and bullhorn BS of "replacement," "groomers," or "crime."

The three parts of the message are we're working hard, they are screwing us over, and this is what we need to do.

This strategy was first successfully tested in the unions, then its first electoral success came in Minnesota in 2018, under the banner 'Greater than Fear.' There, against the odds, progressive multi-racial candidates, including Democratic Governor and 2024 VP pick Tim Walz, won to turn a red state blue[283].

Anat's messaging appears simple (so simple, no one thought of it before!). Here is an example of what we could have seen in the 2024 election:

> "For too long, we have let a group of wealthy elite billionaires, along with their high-priced lobbyists and corrupt politicians, steal the wealth of our work and deny us our freedom to thrive. So it is that Trump and his MAGA politicians, who talk about hardworking Americans, burden us with taxes whilst ensuring that their ultra-rich Wall Street

friends, billionaires, and corporations pay next to nothing. All this is happening whilst we, the true hardworking, patriotic white, black, and brown Americans, were promised that if we worked hard and played by the rules, we would be better off than our parents. It shouldn't be too much to expect a decent education and the training to get us a good job that can pay a mortgage on a home of our own. It shouldn't be too much to expect not to go bankrupt from medical bills, and it shouldn't be too much to expect that when we get older, the taxes we paid should allow us decent healthcare and social security. Instead, Trump and his MAGA Republicans pit us against one another and hope that while we are fighting, we won't notice them ripping away our freedoms and picking our pockets to give themselves more tax cuts. Well, know this: we notice, and we are saying enough is enough. We want to take our country back for every hardworking American of every background in every state. No exceptions."[284]

The beauty of the inclusive Race/Class Narrative is that white folks don't need to be mind readers, because it's right there: *"white, black, and brown."* The inclusiveness is the glue that binds everyone together in progress, and it leaves no room for confusion or doubt, as no one is left out.

Equally important, it also points out who is truly responsible for our problems: the greedy few. If used in 2024, this would have been a nightmare for Republicans, as it goes against everything they have been gaslighting Americans about for the past fifty years. Into the bargain, all the BS talk about 'woke,' CRT, DEI, "Haitians eating pets," and being "replaced" magically loses its power.

If you still doubt me, picture this scenario. It's June 2024, and you start a new job at an air conditioning manufacturer in Arizona where most of the employees are Latino. When you get there, everyone is speaking in Spanish, and no one is speaking to you. You don't understand a word that they are saying, but sometimes they burst out laughing, and as you don't know what they are saying, you wonder whether they are laughing at you.

Your frustration and humiliation at being excluded start to build, and as the day goes on, you feel more and more resentment and contempt—the greatest predictors for the breakdown of any relationship[285]—towards these brown people. *'Why can't they learn English?'* and, *'What are they doing in my country?'*

To add insult to injury, come the end of the day, they go to the bar next door for drinks, but you're not invited. When you get home, you accidentally turn on Fox News, and the scales fall from your eyes as finally, someone tells the 'truth.' Then, come election time, who do you think you are going to vote for?

Now, try this second scenario. You show up at work at the same Arizona factory, and everyone is still speaking Spanish. However, a few guys approach you and, with a smile, introduce themselves in English and ask how you're doing. They even ask if you caught the Cardinals game last night. At lunchtime, they kindly offer you some of their delicious homemade burritos. After work, they invite you to join them for a drink at the bar next door. You get home, feeling fantastic at being included and treated equally, and you can't wait to go back the next day.

The second of those scenarios was the race/class narrative. It works because it's immediately inclusive, making you feel you're in a club with everyone working together to make a better future. Because feelings of kindness, respect, and trust are some of the strongest bonding emotions, they will always crush fear, and, if used, could win elections in 2026 and 2028.

Chapter 13

When Coal Miners Drive Cadillacs.

For liberals, coal miners could still be both real friends and powerful messengers. However, right now, many of them might vote Republican, partly because the GOP isn't telling them they are the enemy. While this chapter is ostensibly about miners, it's also about millions of other potentially winnable rural Americans who feel lost, forgotten, and without hope.

To understand why, let's learn a little about ourselves. Sociologists use the term 'Self-Determination Theory.' Essentially, it posits that, to be happy, people need a purpose, some autonomy, and a community.[286] We all need a purpose to wake up each day and feel like we're making a difference. Then, it's important to have a certain level of autonomy, meaning a say in things and the feeling that we matter. And of course, we all want to feel that we are in a community where we belong and we're safe.

Now imagine the life of a former coal miner living in the foothills of the Appalachian Mountains in eastern Kentucky. Whilst at work, his purpose was to descend into the depths of the mine, working hard to provide a better life for his family. His autonomy lay in knowing that his dangerous work was essential, for it kept America's lights on. And his community consisted of his family and his fellow miners, with whom he shared jokes, laughter, drinks, and stories. Outside of that, there was a wider community of social clubs and local businesses that relied on the mine for their livelihoods.

At this point, we are going to get into some critical thinking by getting inside the miners' brains. As they woke up early to go to work, they would receive a boost of dopamine[287], the reward and motivation chemical that drives people towards achieving goals. In their case, it was closely tied to the meaningful work they did to provide for their families. Then, at work, surrounded by their colleagues, their brains would release oxytocin. This is the "relationship" chemical that we get when we are with our friends or loved ones.[288]

They would also receive endorphins[289]; nature's painkillers, helping them to power through their demanding and life-threatening work. If you've ever felt euphoric after singing, dancing or exerting yourself through exercise, those feelings are partly caused by endorphins[290].

These three chemicals make up the 'Angels Cocktail'[291]. When you see 'happy' people and wonder what their secret is, it's because they have these natural drugs coursing through their veins.

But then the mine closes, and the miners, once respected and on top of the world in their small community, are without work. Their purpose is gone, their autonomy is gone, and the Angel's Cocktail has evaporated, to be replaced by the 'Devil's Cocktail' of cortisol and adrenaline[292]. Having this surging through your body is a guaranteed predictor of poor health outcomes, just some of which are anxiety, depression, weight gain, and mood swings.

To understand more real-world effects of the loss of work and community, let's travel back to the late 1960s and the Vietnam War.

Over the course of the war, over two million young men with an average age of nineteen[293], deployed to the hot, mosquito-infested jungles of Vietnam. There, these American troops (known as GIs) faced immense frustration at being engaged in a form of asymmetrical war the American military had never experienced and had no answer to. For the young servicemen, their discombobulation must have doubled, knowing that, despite dropping more bombs than World War II and Korea combined, winning most battles, and killing over a million of their enemy, the Viet Cong[294], they were losing the war. Then, back home, on the nightly news, regular Americans were seeing war for the first time, and many didn't like what they saw with protests erupting and troops labeled as "baby killers" and "murderers."[295]

To compound the GIs bewilderment, all this was taking place just one generation on from when their fathers and uncles had returned home from Europe and the Pacific, lauded as heroes for wresting the world from the iron grip of fascism.

So, our troops were in Vietnam, seven thousand miles from home, away from their families and friends, in an alien and hostile environment, and every day, their buddies were being maimed and killed—58,000 killed in action and over 300,000 wounded[296]—by a mostly unseen enemy using battle tactics their training had never prepared them for.

Today, the condition that many of the young GIs were suffering from is known as 'post-traumatic stress disorder.' However, it wouldn't be until 1980—a full five years after the war had ended—that PTSD was acknowledged as a valid mental illness[297]. So, with no ability to receive treatment, is it surprising that over half the troops sought to numb the pain of life and death in Vietnam with the sedative effects of marijuana[298]. Then, when their commanding officers prohibited the use of marijuana, their suppliers simply switched to the next readily available sedative: heroin. After all, the war was being fought within the notorious opium production area known as the Burmese (Myanmar) Triangle.

By 1971, reports suggested one in five troops was addicted to heroin[299]. This panicked President Nixon on several levels. Top of his concerns was that the army's drug addiction would lead to a loss in the war. However, his self-serving, conspiracy-laden mind conjured up an even more hideous horror; that of thousands of drug-addicted zombie soldiers coming back to wreak havoc on his 'Silent Majority' America.

Being a master of division and of how to stoke fear, anger, and paranoia, he recognized an opportunity to solidify his electoral advantage by further terrifying an already anxious white America. He juxtaposed blacks and liberals with drugs and offered his voters the iron-clad certainty he would smash down on all of them. So it was that in June 1971, Nixon instituted his fraudulent "War on Drugs." He wouldn't have considered that the troops were self-medicating with drugs to sedate themselves from the irredeemable hell of the jungle. To Richard Milhous Nixon, the disposable and replaceable conscripts were part of Uncle Sam's 'Big Green Fighting Machine,' and their only purpose was 'victory.'

Coming forward to 1999, imagine you live in a deindustrialized town in rural America. Since your steady, decent-paying job disappeared, the pains in your body that you could put out of your mind while you were employed seem so much worse now. It's to be expected; the dopamine is gone, the oxytocin is gone, and the endorphins are gone, and all that's left is the Devil's Cocktail. So, you go down to your trusted local doctor, who prescribes you this new wonder drug called 'OxyContin.'

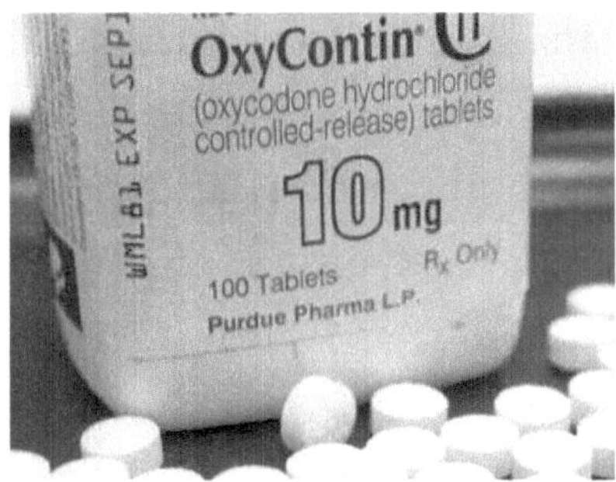

It's been touted as a non-addictive pain reliever that stimulates the release of endorphins, replicating the natural sensations you once experienced. When you take it, even though you're still unemployed, still without prospects, and still without status, for the first time in a long time, life's sharp edges are dulled, and the pain seems to disappear. But to keep that feeling, you need more, so you double the dose, and now life becomes truly blissful.

Just to segue into the matter of drugs. Let's debunk the myth of drug addiction. There is no evidence of this in any peer-reviewed scientific study[300]. This BS comes from the same patriarchal, far-right fools who tell us that marijuana is the gateway drug to heroin. Of course, I have a receipt.

I first learned about the work of Professor Bruce Alexander of Simon Fraser University in British Columbia, Canada, from Johann Hari's epic 2015 book, 'Chasing the Scream', a book about the failure of the war on drugs, but also how connection, not sobriety, is the opposite of addiction.

In the late 1970s, Professor Alexander had been conducting rigorous and realistic lab studies on the life of rats[301]. In one experiment, he put a rat in a cage with nothing to do—no purpose. The creature's only control, or autonomy, was to drink either fresh water or cocaine-laced water. I should add that the rat was all alone—no community. Without purpose, autonomy, or community, the rat drank the cocaine-laced water until it died.

Professor Alexander then reconfigured the test by creating "Rat Park." Here, several rats, who, like humans, are highly social creatures[302], could interact with each other in a controlled play area filled with spinning wheels and obstacles. Within Rat Park, the subjects got the same two bottles of water, one fresh and the other laced with cocaine. The rats tried the cocaine water once, but from then on drank exclusively from the fresh water bottle. It was because these sentient beings had purpose, autonomy, and community that they didn't need to self-medicate.

Some may think rats don't provide a suitable sample study, so consider something else. Every year, over fifty million people across America, of all ages, genders, and races, undergo hospital procedures[303]. Following their procedures, many patients receive pharmaceutical-grade morphine through an intravenous drip. According to the National Institute of Health, morphine is half as potent as pure heroin[304].

However, pure morphine is still stronger than the heroin you will receive if you are unlucky enough to need to buy it from an illegal dealer, as that street heroin will have been 'cut' with substances like baking soda, powdered milk, or cheap painkillers to make it more profitable for the dealer. Because of this, its strength is only around half that of morphine and a little over one-third of pure heroin[305].

Notwithstanding all that, there is not a single recorded case of any hospital patient ever becoming addicted to drugs after receiving post-procedure morphine. To paint a picture, no one's grandma ever left the ER after her hip replacement demanding that grandpa go find a dealer to hook her up with a fix of heroin.

Still not convinced? Then recall how scared Nixon was about the potential threat posed by the returning zombie soldiers to his 'silent majority' voters. As a result, in 1974, the Department of Defense commissioned a study on returning GIs. The highly regarded psychiatric researcher, Lee Robins, carried it out. The findings revealed that in Vietnam, 34% of troops had used heroin, and 20% were addicted to it. However, upon coming home to America, addiction rates among these troops plummeted by a staggering 95%.

The one in five troops addicted to heroin in Vietnam decreased to a mere one in a hundred once they came home[306]. *Home* was the magic word, because home was where they felt safe, and home was where their families were, and at home, no one was trying to kill them.

Unfortunately, coming forward to present times, up in the mountains, down in the creeks, and across the prairies of rural America, the pain started, and it never went away.

In the case of the coal miners, the jobs never came back, their kids left for better opportunities, and their communities crumbled. And they were left behind, and *home* was now the place where all the problems were. Then, 2016 came around, and a bombastic orange New York conman came to their forgotten flyover town, put on a hard hat, and mimed digging coal, and they dug him.

He told them that he would make them kings again, and they thought that finally someone saw them and saw the real reason behind their pain. Thus, with hope, they cast their votes, but then nothing changed.

So, they, and many other desperate rural Americans, kept on medicating to relieve the pain of just being alive. Then, when their doctor cut off their OxyContin—which was always just heroin in a designer dress—a dealer stepped in to supply them with real heroin, and when heroin stopped hitting the mark, that same dealer introduced them to the perilous allure of fentanyl. In it, they were experiencing a drug that offers nirvanic levels of blissful serenity, but at fifty times the potency of heroin. Just taking it meant gambling with their lives. But still they took it, because....*anything to make the pain go away*[307].

Trump sold miners a lie that he was going to reinvigorate their mines and their communities. Yet, more coal mines closed in his first term than in Obama's[308]. Today, there are just 40,000 coal miners left[309]. For Democrats, who need all the friends they can get, these are 40,000 decent, valuable men and women with a proud history of helping to build America. However, imagine the coal miner watching Fox or Newsmax and hearing about the future of electric cars, solar power, wind turbines, and battery storage, and it's a future that they're excluded from.

So, when deviant GOP devils come around peddling their simple, seductive lies, these folks are receptive. Miners don't vote GOP because they are stupid. Most know that Republicans may be terrible, but at least they offer some hope of keeping the mine open; and if you've ever been in love with someone who didn't love you back, you'll know all about the power of hope.

Still, it's a near certainty that the future will be a time when homes, industry, and vehicles will all run on electricity. However, before we get there, it's not just coal miners who are threatened.

Wherever new technology challenges the old, the old will resist. Thus, the same planet-heating corporations that lie and cheat to prop up their failing endeavors will never sleep while there is someone to fleece. To this point, allow me to take you on a small sojourn through some of their ruinously expensive and irredeemably useless ideas to get rid of the 6.3 billion tons of annual US carbon emissions[310] .

We can start with carbon capture and storage (CCS). In this con, fossil-fuel power stations take the pollution that would otherwise go into the air and store it underground. It's completely unproven, incredibly complicated, and exceedingly expensive. Yet, for proponents of CCS, it's a super grift. After all, it's the 'rubes' (taxpayers and utility bill payers) who will pay for it.

CCS is focused on the 12,000 power stations in America[311]. According to the Environmental Protection Agency (EPA), they are responsible for one quarter of domestic emissions[312]. The cost of CCS is around $200 per ton[313].

My non-Nobel Laureate mathematics tells me that the cost of cleaning up 1.6 billion tons of power station pollution would be $320 billion.

Remember, that was just for a quarter of emissions. For the other three-quarters (vehicles, factories, gas boilers, cows, and Californian wildfires), the fossil fuel crowd has Direct Air Capture (DAC). Think of the lunacy of a gigantic, energy-gobbling air purifier trying to suck up all the air *outside* your house.

Our friends at the International Energy Agency inform us this completely unproven technology can cost a stroke-inducing $800 per ton[314].

Again with the calculator. We need to capture those 4.7 billion tons of Co2. Don't worry, it'll only cost $3.8 trillion a year; nothing serious, just two-thirds of the federal budget!

As to the scale of construction of all this nonsense. In 2023, out of the 12,000 power stations, only fifteen are using CCS[315]. As far as DAC goes, there's just one facility in operation, and it sucks a measly 1000 tons of carbon[316]. For reference, that's like levying a $1,000 fine on a billionaire like Mad Musk.

Then, we must ask, where are the engineers going to come from to build the other 11,985 CCS facilities? Or the other 4.7 million DAC facilities?

These fossil-fuel-friendly ideas have all flown in from cloud cuckoo land. Yet the incompetent corporate media never bothers questioning them. Please don't take my word for it. Here's Stanford University's Professor of Civil and Environmental Engineering, Professor Mark Jacobson, speaking to the London Guardian;

> Carbon capture and storage is solely designed to keep the fossil fuel industry in business," he says. Only some of the CO2 is captured and buried, he says, and deadly air pollution continues unabated. Blue hydrogen, produced from fossil gas with some CO2 then captured and buried, is far inferior to green hydrogen produced directly from renewable electricity, Jacobson says: "Blue hydrogen is just really convoluted.[317]

I can hear some liberal friends say that I should talk about generating more clean energy from nuclear power. We can. Today, one-fifth of US energy comes from nuclear power[318]. The problem with this is that the word after 'nuclear' in most people's minds is always 'bomb.' Cue world destruction and the end of humanity.

Then, there's the fear of a nuclear plant meltdown. I know that the effects of fossil fuel pollution are much worse and kill over five million people a year. However, as it's a silent, unseen killer, the deaths are impossible to visualize[319].

However, a meltdown at a nuclear reactor is visceral. Think of Three Mile Island, Chernobyl, or Fukushima. To aid all this, Americans have had thirty-five years of seeing the work of Homer Simpson, the incompetent nuclear safety inspector at the Springfield Nuclear Plant, in the fictional Simpsons TV show. You may scoff, but we know stories sit in people's minds, and millions more folks will have seen the Springfield Plant than will ever know of the rigorous safety regime that takes place at a real nuclear plant.

Other downsides of nuclear are the enormous costs and the protracted build times. Unit 3 at Plant Vogtle, Georgia, is the latest nuclear project to be completed. Started in 2009, this six-year project took fourteen years to complete, and originally budgeted at $14 billion, it ended up costing $31 billion[320].

Even if people are still boosting nuclear, there's the matter of disposing of the radioactive waste and of the reactor's potential as a terrorist target.

However, some of my biggest doubts about nuclear as a future savior are down to the fractional number of jobs that it creates. The hundred working reactors across the US only employ 100,000 people[321].

Now that we have walked past the funhouse mirror that reflects insanity back as salvation, there's a window and an opportunity to win over most Americans.

CLIMATE RESCUE CORPS

It was Democratic messaging guru Billy Ray who told us to ditch doomsday talk of "climate catastrophe" and "human extinction" and instead talk about 'Climate Rescue'[322]. All I've done is build upon those words. So, it is that I envisage the people working in these new energy industries will be part of the 'Climate Rescue Corps.' Every day, they can take pride in knowing that their work is invaluable, both in keeping America's lights on and in making the future better for their own grandchildren.

Here is where miners can become our messengers. As the future is about to kill their industry, we must thank them for what they have done and explain that coal will go, but it will be replaced in their communities with wind, solar, and battery storage. As far as mining goes, within America, there are plentiful reserves of soda ash and lithium for batteries and neodymium for EV motors[323].

As regards solar energy, this will be one of the largest components of climate rescue. Indeed, today, vast solar farms are being built, like the $1.4 billion, 550-megawatt Desert Sunlight farm in California[324]. Set across 4100 acres, it will provide power for 160,000 homes.

Here's where we reach a problem with solar. There are nearly twenty thousand incorporated places (towns and cities) across the nation. Fifteen thousand of them have under five thousand residents. Indeed, five thousand towns have under five hundred residents[325].

Building mega solar plants far away from residents won't win over enough people in those fifteen thousand small towns whose votes decide elections. So, as every smart politician knows, we go local.

The Bureau of Land Management estimates the land required for all the solar panels needed to decarbonize the American energy sector at twenty-two million acres[326]. If that sounds like a lot, bear in mind America is over two billion acres, 40% of which is farmland[327]. So it is that farmers can become our friends and benefit from the new energy revolution.

Personally, I'm thinking of 200-acre (one hundred football fields) solar and wind farms that will bring hope and pride to local folks. After all, they will be the people working there. Also, this way, every town and county gets to benefit.

This electricity will be used by local residents, but to incentivize them, it's vitally important that it's cheap. After all, the future must be better than the past. Which means cheaper electricity.

At all costs, we need to avoid jumping out of the fire and into the frying pan by allowing private equity jackals anywhere near this. These critters would want a 90% return and jack up the residents' bills just to pay for their private jets. Therefore, it's an idea to look to federal or municipal bonds or mutual and pension funds for funding. For them, a steady return from customers who always need electricity would be a dream investment.

Remember the cloud-cuckoo craziness you read previously about the cost of carbon capture. Well, to illustrate the basic economics of renewable energy, we have a receipt from the highly respected Lawrence Berkeley National Laboratory. It reports each year on the cost of solar. In 2022, non-subsidized utility-scale solar was only $0.04 per kilowatt hour, and it's falling every year[328].

To make this work, it's essential that the customer never pays more than $0.10 per kilowatt hour. This means that an electric car could travel 100 miles for under $3[329], and even a heavy electric Ford F-150 Lightning could cover those 100 miles for just $5[330].

For the excess production of energy, there are opportunities to make other fuels like 'green hydrogen' (by heating water to separate the hydrogen and oxygen molecules).

Alongside these sites will be the battery storage for nighttime electricity. Also, fracking technology can pump water into underground reservoirs and release it at night to spin turbines to create more electricity.

Unlike the moronic carbon capture pipe dream, all the technology for these new industries exists today. Then, while we're saving humanity, the new industries will create millions of new jobs, just some of which will be electricians, engineers, installers, and delivery drivers[331].

Once the renewables are pumping out clean energy in communities all across the nation, business and industry will come, and where there is industry, there will be workers, and those workers will need new homes.

This means a market for affordable, energy-efficient, world-class, American-made modular homes built in new local factories. Those homes will run on electricity and so will need American-made heat pumps.

Then, to service all these communities, there will be shops, restaurants, and schools. Thus, job after job after job will be created, all to help rebuild the American middle class. This plan not only shows Democrats helping, it shows the government helping, and it helps save your grandchildren. What it also says to our friends that we have never met in places that we have never been is, 'We'll never leave you behind.'

If that doesn't move liberals, then act in your own self-interest. The friends in those fifteen thousand small towns are the heartland. You will read in the next chapter how the day is coming when they will have complete control of the Senate, and I'm certain they will remember who didn't help them.

Should my powers of persuasion still leave you unconvinced, then consider this. You may understand the devastating effects of undertaking the most reckless, uncontrolled scientific experiment in human history.

You may also grasp an inkling of the seething hell we will face in moving from 1.5 degrees of planetary warming to 2 or 2.5 degrees. If so, you can probably join the dots and connect it all to more frequent floods, firestorms. heatwaves, and hurricanes.

The really bright among you will know it's less a problem for the planet than it is for us puny humans. And if you think that you're not puny, try standing in a hurricane, swimming in a storm surge, or working outdoors in fifty-degree heat. This will become the norm, because the people who you need to reach in order to win those Senate seats either don't know or, more likely, aren't listening.

Self-interest tells us we have to make it worth our rural friend's interest to gain their interest. So give them a job and the cheap energy that makes them look forward to the new hopeful future.

There really isn't any need to talk about 'Co2,' 'parts per million,' or 'net zero' to these folks. As long as they are making America great by working in the new energy industries of wind and solar and then using that cheap local electricity to fuel their electric vehicles and homes, we'll be well on the way to solving the problem. Indeed, hopefully one day, coal miners will drive (electric) Cadillacs.

Chapter 14

How To Turn A Red State Blue.

When you think of red states—which are in fact mostly the rural areas of those states—especially after the 2024 election, images may form in your mind of pickup-driving gun-wielding crazies, demonic fake-Christian pastors, and calamitous natural disasters. Of course, I must never forget the shameless hypocrites masquerading as politicians who force women to give birth to their rapists' babies, suppress the vote, allow guns everywhere, and ban transgender folks.

Maybe you have a radicalized relative from there and despise having to hear their hate-filled, Fox-fed talking points. I understand how easy it might seem to just throw these places and their people away, but that way, as we have seen, we all lose.

I was lucky to meet some kind and beautiful people from the South a long time ago, and it taught me how many friends there are that we've never met in places that we've never been. Today, it's them who suffer in states like Florida, Missouri, Texas, and Tennessee.

Back in 1999, beset by the ignorance of the uninformed, I envisaged 'the Deep South' as some forbidding neo-Confederate Gothic horror zone where one's demise might arise as the result of multitudinous murderous mechanisms; Hollywood has a lot to answer for.

My lesson in reality came through a chance encounter with a young couple from Louisiana who I met at that year's New Year's Eve celebrations in Times Square, New York. They invited me to Louisiana the next year.

This was nearly twenty-five years ago, in the sunset days of Bill Clinton's presidency. Just a week before I got there, the Supreme Court had called the election for George W. Bush.

No one could have known, but it was also the twilight of the age of American innocence. Within nine months, nineteen extreme conservative religious fundamentalists would board three planes to murder that innocence, and in doing so, irrevocably reshape the course of world history. However, whilst I was there, that was all in a future universe, far removed from my imagination.

Instead, one abiding memory was a road trip from Louisiana to Georgia to see a college football game. As we drove through Mississippi and Alabama, my mind struggled to reconcile the paradox of the richest nation in human history also being the home to shanty shacks and extreme poverty.

Later on, I would learn the answer to that question, but whilst there, in that completely unfamiliar environment, I embraced the differences that make life so special. I was so lucky to be taken around by David and Dana, for what was normal to them was, to me, an outsider, a treasure trove of experiences and memories.

I recall Dana's Uncle Brent. A veteran who, literally, lived in a cabin in the woods with rabbits hanging on the porch. Hollywood couldn't make him up. I'm not exaggerating when I tell you that he met us with a shotgun in one hand and a beer in the other. But I didn't care, as he was a decent and generous man. Like I said, millions of friends that you've never met, in places that you've never been.

To the matter of those places, when the founding fathers set up this constitutional democracy, they favored land over people. They also favored slave states by allowing them to count their enslaved folk as three-fifths of a white man. From this, we got the imperfect electoral college and also the Senate. Today, whether you are half a million people in Wyoming or forty million in California, you only get two senators. And we know, in 2024, with the current 51-49 Senate split, how difficult it is to govern with a small majority.

But it can get harder. With the increasing urbanization of America, a huge transformation is taking place that, if left unaddressed, means that a future Democratic administration can kiss goodbye to any legislation they hope to enact.

Remember what you read about those fifteen thousand small towns in the last chapter? Well, back in 2017, the Washington Post reported a study from Baruch College that found that, by 2040, it is quite possible that nearly three-quarters of the US population will live in just fifteen states. As a result, those voters will only have thirty out of the hundred Senate seats.

The remaining one-third of the population will live in thirty-five, mostly rural states, but will have seventy out of one hundred senators. In those states, the residents will be older, whiter, and more conservative. Indeed, today, three-quarters of rural America are white[332]. Now, kindly explain to me how you win a future election without getting some of these folks on board?[333]

Fortunately, this chapter will help you understand where our red and rural cousins live and ways to win over enough of them to turn some of these states blue.

Later on, we will talk more about the Senate, but for now, if liberals ever want to effect real change, it's time to stop thinking about Congress and start understanding the state legislatures. After all, it was the legislatures of the eleven Confederate states that, back in 1861, voted to secede and nearly killed the United States.

Today, it's in state legislatures where America's real laws are made. This is where red-state Republicans pass laws to ruin lives, all without any meaningful challenge from the federal government. The legislatures rule on everything from abortion rights, voting rights, healthcare, and gun control to whether trans kids can actually exist. How powerful these places are is neatly illustrated by the supremacy of American law. Federal law supersedes state law, but a state constitution supersedes federal law.

This is why state-wide direct democracy ballot measures are so important. As an example, since Roe v. Wade was overturned, across mostly red state America, citizens have been fighting for the chance to enshrine a woman's right to choose in their state constitutions. To date, voters in Kansas, Kentucky, and Ohio have all succeeded. By doing so, they ensure an absolute right to their own privacy and protection.

Today, common wisdom is that red/rural states are red because they want to be red, but what if they're red because no one ever went to meet them, listen to them, and make friends? To this point, in the 2022 midterms, fifteen red states had over 40% of their state legislature seats uncontested. That's 1600 seats where no Democrat was even on the ballot[334].

There are a couple of points to bear in mind here. On the same ballot where voters put a X next to the state rep's name are also the names for candidates in the House and Senate races. But why would an independent or Republican-leaning voter ever put an X next to the Democrats' name when they have never seen or heard from any Democrats?

There's more. The state legislature, which Dems leave uncontested, draws the voter maps for both itself and the congressional races. So, even if Democrats now want to stand, GOP gerrymandering ensures that their race will be twice as hard.

For an example of what the tip of the MAGA spear looks like, we can travel to Tennessee, the Volunteer State. There, the state legislature, with its GOP supermajority, is completely unaccountable. In common with other GOP state legislatures, it has outlawed abortion, gutted public school education, suppressed the vote, criminalized trans folks, and allowed guns everywhere. Oh, and that supermajority means that even though Democrats turn up in the legislature, their votes never matter.

You might think that the states' 'ignorant, Fox-News-viewing' people get what they vote for. But know this: even today, Tennessee votes over one-third Democratic. That's one in three Tennesseans as your friends. It's the home of, among many others, the brilliant 'Liberal Redneck,' Trey Crowder, and the inspirational Tennessee Brando, as well as an up-and-coming young singer called Taylor Swift.

In the state legislature, hardworking progressives like Justin Pearson, Justin Jones, Aftyn Behn, and Gloria Johnson are fighting for Tennesseans' rights. Yet, shockingly, in the 2022 elections, Democrats left nearly half of the seats for the state legislature uncontested[335].

Here's where the rubber hits the road. In 2024, Democrats lost the West Virginia Senate seat and needed to make up that loss elsewhere. Gloria Johnson stood in Tennessee against the Trump-loving Marsha Blackburn. Gloria is a deeply committed progressive candidate. However, brilliant as she undoubtedly was, she faced an uphill battle considering that across half the state, voters never got to hear about the innumerable ways the Democratic administration was helping to make their lives better.

If we head to the next state over, we get to beautiful Missouri, the Show Me State. We can meet Jess Piper, the co-executive director of Blue Missouri, a grassroots organization dedicated to supporting candidates in the state legislature races of Missouri. She is also the host of the invaluable Dirt Road Democrats podcast. Over the next six paragraphs, be prepared to learn what a three-year political science degree at Yale University wouldn't teach you.

Jess stood for a state legislature seat in Missouri's 1st Congressional District in 2022 and won 25% with no Democratic Legislative Campaign Committee (DLCC) support and only small-dollar donations. This was a seat that had been uncontested since 2014. She summarized a situation that might make you want to pull your hair out;

> I'll tell you what it looks like. We're training progressives to
> vote for Republicans, because every time I go to the ballot

and there's no one to vote for, I pull a Republican ticket. I vote in the Republican primaries because I'm gonna vote for the person who is least likely to hurt me. And we have trained a generation of Democrats and progressives to vote for Republicans. And that's awful, and that's what we're up against. You have places in the Boot Hill that haven't had a Democrat for 30 years.[336]

Jess spoke about the advantages of just having a Democrat standing for election. For her race, she raised $25,000 in small-dollar donations. That forced her lazy GOP opponent to pony up $100,000 of his own money—that he could otherwise have used to prop up a failing fellow GOP candidate.

As to that cost of saving democracy, political strategist Michelle Hornish, who also works with 'Blue Missouri,' emphasized that as little as $5000 can cover the expenses for a Democratic candidate to run a campaign for a state house seat in one of these currently uncontested districts[337].

Equally important as forcing the GOP to spend money, these candidates are talking to voters who watch Fox, Newsmax, or OAAN, and never hear about the mismanagement by the GOP state government. After all, it's the state that handles the school budgets, local hospitals, potholed roads, and property taxes. In Jess Piper's race, her opponent knew he could never talk about the issues because the GOP didn't care about them. Instead, all he prattled on about was 'Biden,' CRT, and 'woke.'

To the point of why he could do that, Jess hit us with another bombshell that 99% of liberals don't understand about voting in rural America.

What happened is, Democrats pulled out of rural places. There is no party. The GOP has also pulled out, but I'll say this, they already have built-in organizations, because they have a bunch of churches. So, my little town of 480 people has four churches, with at least two of these churches organizing for GOP values. They are pro-life, they are pro Second Amendment. They feel like their values align with the GOP. So, the Republicans don't have to come into my space because the churches are organizing for them. But when I talk to rural Americans about their actual values, about economic issues and that sort of thing, they always align with the De mocrats.[338]

Remember, too, that these places aren't Saccarine Sweet Sacramento. This is dirt-road territory, where some houses have double-sided flags outside that say, "FUCK BIDEN AND FUCK YOU FOR VOTING FOR HIM!" (Amazon 2024: $21.99)[339].

Now consider that people like Jess are often alone and outnumbered, and imagine the determination and grit they must have to stand as a candidate. Then throw into the mix that these are also 'authentic' and 'genuine' folks whose lived experience mirrors the people in their districts. With some funding and organization, they could have won and helped to bring progressive issues to red states.

Even if you're still not down with all this state legislature malarkey, just know, while people like Jess are out there spreading the Democratic message, they are also acting as pathfinders for future Democratic House and Senate candidates.

The great campaigner and documentary filmmaker, Michael Moore, came at the rural voter issue from a slightly different angle. He had a phrase to win back red/rural America. He imagined a service called "DEMOCRATS HELP."[340] Stuck in the snow? call DEMOCRATS HELP. Fence needs fixing? Call DEMOCRATS HELP. Need a lift to the Doctor? Call DEMOCRATS HELP.

Some people might scoff at this, but then they are also the ones who call every election wrong and don't even bother standing candidates in many red or rural seats.

Thinking about that leads me to a character who was completely incapable of seeing how helping people and showing empathy was a surefire way to win votes. Billionaire Michael Bloomberg wasted an eye-watering $90 million in the 2020 Democratic presidential primary to secure just 20% of the votes[341].

During COVID, imagine if he had invested that money in a "DEMOCRATS HELP" style initiative in rural areas. He could even have used his own name for the projects, like The Bloomberg Food Pantry, The Bloomberg Rural Bus Service, The Bloomberg Pothole Fixers, The Bloomberg Home Help Service, and The Bloomberg Rural Clinic. I guarantee he would have gotten more than 20% in the next Democratic primary.

But, of course, that ground game was not in his self-interest, as he's far too important to deal with the 'little people.' Instead, he squandered the $90 million on D.C. consultants, who puffed up his ego with expensive TV ads, and so, from his ivory tower, all he accomplished was to showcase his excessive wealth and misguided priorities.

To see the polar opposite of Mr. Bloomberg, we can meet former State Senator Chloe Maxmin, an inspiring, dynamic, young, and authentic candidate from Maine, the most rural state in the nation.

Chloe won two tough conservative rural seats (Trump +16) for both the Maine House of Representatives in 2018 and the State Senate in 2020. Together with her best friend and campaign manager, Canyon Woodward, they wrote a book about their experiences entitled 'Dirt Road Revival: How to Rebuild Rural Politics and Why Our Future Depends on It.'

Canyon described the first 2018 campaign. They understood that the Democrats' rural problem was having "Ikea candidates" who weren't "authentic." The DLCC offered them campaign money, but only if they followed the consultant class orthodoxy.

Just as a point of note, the political consultant's job is to shepherd a candidate to victory. They advise on tactics and strategy. Yet, many of these "West Wing"-style people have never held a proper job or bothered to listen to a rural voter. Their principal talents are to waste the candidates' money on boring direct mail and expensive TV ads. As a side hustle, they can water down and neuter any progressive messaging—that would be messaging about things like healthcare, union rights, sick leave, and family leave—you know, all the things that are popular among voters.

Back to Maine. The Maxmin campaign turned down the DLCC money. Canyon says;

> Getting handed down a budget by Democratic leadership, they wanted us to spend about two-thirds of our budget on their consultants to run a direct mail campaign; you know those awful mailers that we all get and toss immediately into the trash and so we rejected that and instead just designed everything ourselves.[342]

Instead of wasting money on consultants, Chloe knocked on thousands of doors, engaging with voters, and would write a thank-you "Clincher Card" after each of her visits. That personal touch resonated with folks who had previously felt overlooked (translation: 'left behind'), making them feel valued and heard. To that exact point, when she went to canvass a rural man living in a trailer, he said to her;

> You're the first person to listen to me. Everyone judges what
> my house looks like. They don't bother to knock. I'm grateful
> that you came. I'm going to vote for you.[343]

In campaigning, she was also careful to avoid complicated wonkish jargon; remember, hers was a rural Republican +16 district. Instead of giving them the national party line, she listened to her voters. In her words;

> I live in a very rural natural resources-based community, and
> we don't really talk about climate change, we don't really talk
> about green jobs, but everything I heard was, "We want good
> jobs, we want growing industries, we want to protect our
> natural resources, we want to lower our property taxes, and
> we want to make sure that we're really boosting vocational
> training and technical training.[344]

Without the need to enter the mostly useless world of consultants, pollsters, or focus groups, here are real people explaining exactly how to win their votes: just make their lives better.

Chloe Maxmin's hard work paid off and won her a seat in the state house in 2018, with an eleven-point swing from the losing Dem in 2016. Bear in mind, this rural-red seat had just been left there for the GOP to pick up.

Once in the legislature, Chloe didn't forget her voters and played a pivotal role in successfully passing a groundbreaking Green New Deal for Maine.

Come 2020, she stood for the state senate. Her election platform centered on the idea of 'Politics as Public Service,' aiming to assist all voters by advocating for universal healthcare, rural broadband, and green jobs. She won, with a 51% to 49% win over the incumbent Republican. Her words, again, are instructive;

Every year we keep electing the same kind of folks,"_"They tell us the same things, they act the same way, we elect them, they get into the state House, and they break the same promises and we're left with the same disillusionment that we had before.[345]

Chloe didn't stand for re-election, but she had laid the foundations for another progressive local Democrat to carry the torch; Cameron Reny, a working-class local educator, won the seat in 2022[346].

Given all you've just read, now let's look at the 2020 Maine Senate race between Republican Susan Collins and Democrat Sara Gideon. Despite the Democrats holding majorities in the Maine House and Senate, and the Democratic Senatorial Campaign Committee (DSCC) raising a campaign war chest of over $69 million, Mrs. Gideon only secured 42% of the vote[347].

The campaign is worth examining, for it was a model of how to lose a race. Gideon's donor-friendly, 'moderate' platform rejected both the Green New Deal and Universal Health Care[348]. These were two policies that Chloe Maxim showed were popular when she put a Maine face on them. Gideon might as well have just told the voters that she didn't care.

It gets worse. Mrs. Gideon's husband was a meritocratic multimillion-aire lawyer whose law firm benefited from millions of dollars of the federal government, PPP loan-forgiveness intended to prop-up small businesses.

What this debacle of a campaign proved was that voters want authentic candidates who will fight for them. Ironically, Gideon's Democratic primary rival, Bre Kidman, supported popular progressive policies, such as a $15 minimum wage, universal healthcare, education, and green jobs. However, Ms. Kidman rejected corporate donor funds for costly TV advertisements and instead prioritized engaging with and listening to the voters. Unsurprisingly, the DSCC said, 'No thanks,' and didn't support her.

The fiercely smart Ms. Kidman gave us a forensic insight into Gideon's loss, the party elite, and the consultant class:

> The model this cycle — and the model I am certain we'll see repeated as Chuck Schumer continues on as Minority Leader — is that the party chooses a candidate they expect to bring in money, a candidate who will go along with corporate interests that fund the legions of Democratic campaign professionals that keep the machine running. Mainers could smell the disingenuousness a mile away and, frankly, I don't think the top-dollar, out-of-state consultants who worked on the campaign did anything at all to mask it.[349]

Something those consultants never grasp about winning people over leads us to another simple way to make friends of red and rural voters: healthcare. We all know that nothing is more important to us than our health, so what message does it send to rural America that they don't even merit a hospital?

Yet, the Center for Healthcare Quality and Payment Reform (CHQPR) found that, for lack of state funds, over six hundred rural hospitals are at risk of closing in 2023[350]. That's nearly one in three rural hospitals.

The states these hospitals are closing in are all red, and all their GOP state legislatures rejected the FREE federal government money from the Affordable Care Act that would have staffed and maintained the hospitals[351].

For Democrats, messaging this should be as easy as bench-pressing a can of Pringles. Remember that bit about caring for people? It's a strength, not a weakness. Obviously, I have a receipt. This, from Harold Miller, President of the CHQPR:

> In many of the smallest rural communities, the only thing there is the hospital. The hospital is the only source. Not only is it the only emergency department and the only source of inpatient care, it's the only source of laboratory services, the only place to get an X-ray or radiology. It may even be the only place where there is primary care.[352]

We can now move on to someone who might need a hospital. In those red and rural areas, there are two million small family farms, making up nine out of ten of all US farms[353]. These are the folks who work nearly 40% of the landmass of America. The majority work on farms of under five hundred acres, doing the hard work of raising beef and chicken and growing corn, soybeans, and wheat.

Sadly, despair amongst small family farmers is rife. Male farmer suicide rates are three times higher than the national average[354]. There are a combination of reasons for this. We can start with the old idea of self-reliant, mostly Republican-voting men who don't talk about their feelings. Then, there is the stress of having to deal with toxic, monopolistic, Republican-donating Big Ag[355], looking to rip them off in the purchases of seed, fertilizer, and machines, and also dictate how low a price they pay for the farmers produce[356].

Many liberals will rail against these land-rich but cash poor farmers[357] for voting against their own interests. But what if a solution to farmers' hopelessness and despair lay in the hope and opportunity that could also help liberals? As we have read, we want to roll out solar, wind, green hydrogen and energy storage industries in every corner of America. We know we need 22 million acres, or 1% of the American landmass.

With farmers working on 879 million acres, there is an opportunity for them to lease or sell some of their land to the new industries[358]. This would not only offer them a guaranteed revenue but also provide them with cheap electricity to power their machines and farms.

To wrap up, nothing you have read over the past two chapters is rocket science. We just start by helping red and rural folks to make their lives better by bringing cheap energy, creating good-paying local jobs, and ensuring local healthcare. Following on from that, and using a policy you will read about in the next chapter, in 2028, we can turn many red states blue.

Chapter 15

How To Win Every Election

There is an immutable law of politics. Voters don't want to hear about the good things that were done yesterday; they want to hear about the good things that are coming tomorrow. That's what hope is, and that's what will win over a small portion of GOP voters and get many more of the 90 million non-voters[359] to show up.

In 2020, a massive Medill School of Journalism/NPR/Ipsos survey of non-voters gave us an insight into their reasons for not voting. 72% offered either not being registered to vote, not being interested, or not liking the candidates. One 58-year-old woman from North Carolina said, "Me and my friends don't talk about politics much because politicians have no idea what's going on in our lives."[360]

In 2016, the Knight Foundation, in their 100 Million Project, commissioned one of the largest studies of chronic non-voters and found very similar reasons[361]. Don't blame them; many citizens are low information and low interest, and it's our job to break through their 'attention filters' and make them enthusiastic.

For most people, voting is about feelings, and as far as feelings go, nothing makes them feel better than receiving cash. Money talks, money moves minds, and money is the easiest way to make people like the government.

There is a policy that will win over millions of non-voters and energize existing voters while putting the GOP on permanent defense. It's also the fastest method to make friends with a lot of Americans who, put euphemistically, may not be that friendly to us today. It's an entitlement, and I'll stake everything I own that they will fight anyone who tries to stop them from getting it.

So, let's see who we're talking about winning over. According to a 2023 US Census Bureau survey of incomes, one-third of American workers, or 63 million people, earn less than $25,000 a year[362]. However, we want to have the widest pool of beneficiaries, so let's expand that out to all American workers earning less than $65,000 per year. Now we're up to nearly two-thirds of all workers, or a whopping 155 million people[363]. Then, to really cement the deal, we add in the sixty-five million seniors and nine million veterans. This brings us to 229 million Americans, or two out of every three citizens.

I wanted nothing complicated, so the plan doesn't involve anything they had to claim or apply for. The inspiration was the COVID stimulus payments. I came up with the 'THANK YOU AMERICAN WORKERS PAYMENT,' or TAWP.

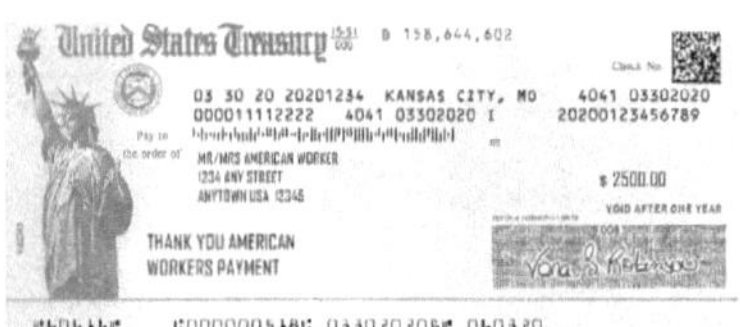

It's a $2500 payment (call it a tax credit if you need to pass it as legislation) to those 229 million American workers (and potential voters), to be paid every year, just like the stimulus check. The cost would be $572 billion, or about half of the defense budget.

If I may gently remind you that in 2024, 74 million people voted Democratic. The $2500 TAWP will obviously energize many of them. However, it will also help to win over the 155 million people who didn't vote Democratic but now have 2500 reasons to do so.

Should you be skeptical about the popularity of this, just know that during COVID, the IRS made over 476 million stimulus payments, totaling

$814 billion to citizens[364]. According to a 2020 Morning Consult poll, 80% of voters supported these direct payments[365].

The payments were part of the CARES Act of 2022, pushed by Congressional Democrats. However, in a masterful act of self-publicity, in the bottom left corner of the checks was printed: "ECONOMIC IMPACT PAYMENT: PRESIDENT DONALD J TRUMP."

I remember hearing the influential host of the national radio show The Breakfast Club, 'Chalamagne tha God,' speaking on CNN, explaining the political value of these checks, especially to urban folks;

> Like American government has ignored them. And all of a sudden you start getting checks in the mail one day. The stimulus checks, what they call stimis in the hood, for $1,200. And this man's name is on them, Donald Trump. For the first time in probably forever, you just simply feel seen, and you can talk to your next-door neighbor about actually receiving something from the American government.[366]

As far as I can tell, not one payment was ever returned, because the fact is, everyone loves free money. As an instant concrete foundation to rebuild the Democratic brand across the nation, the TAWP has no rival. It would also act as a political bulletproof vest against which GOP BS bullets would just bounce off.

In February 2024, our friends at the conservative Newsweek Magazine provided another receipt with the headline "Biden Sending More Direct Payments to Americans Is Worrying Republicans." This was just after the administration announced it might be expanding the Child Tax Credit for low earners. Chuck Grassley, the wily, ninety-year-old GOP Senator for Iowa, showed the acute political instincts that had won him seven successive Senate terms when he was quoted as saying, "I think passing a tax bill that makes the president look good mailing out checks before the election means he could be re-elected."[367]

As it turned out, President Biden being re-elected wouldn't be a worry for the GOP. Parenthetically, in December 2024, the former president came to understand the power of messaging. Speaking at the Washington-based Brookings Institution, he offered this;

> "I signed the American Rescue Plan, the most significant economic recovery package in our history, and also learned something from Donald Trump…He signed checks for people for 7,400 bucks … and I didn't. Stupid."[368]

To any Democratic strategist still puzzled at how to win, let's return to Charlamagne; "People wonder why folks keep bringing up these stimulus checks. Because it's something that they could actually touch and see. People like cash; cash rules."[369]

With the TAWP, Dems would have something that smashed through people's attention filters and gave them hope. To pass the TAWP, we would only require fifty-one senators and budget reconciliation, just like the 2021 and 2022 budgets. It would have the effect of an immediate cash injection into people's pockets thanks to THE GOVERNMENT. The GOP would scream about 'Marxism' and 'socialism,' and The Heritage Foundation would take time off from murdering American democracy to wheel out some overpaid ghoul to tell the never-ask-a-follow-up-question corporate media that it will bankrupt America.

That part about "socialism" and not being able to afford things is a large part of the reason brilliant ideas like Medicare for All never get off the ground; once the media and pundits hear the GOP scream the word "socialism" a thousand times, they blindly accept that the policy will be too costly. None of this is helped by liberals speaking their own special language, 'wonkish,' and never fighting for what they believe in. So it is, their brilliant ideas wither on the vine.

The TAWP changes all this, and makes life much easier for no-fight liberals. It will act as a bridge that connects the America of poor healthcare, struggling families and debt with the new America of infinite possibilities. Now, we have 229 million white, black and brown Americans seeing THE GOVERNMENT as a friend.

And this doesn't even get on to how it boosts the economy. With that extra $2500 a year, people can buy, save and invest. And whilst they are doing all that, the American worker, who is providing them with all their goods and services, is also earning money they can spend.

How does the GOP fight this? These demons have spent years hoodwinking their voters with bullshit three-letter cultural issues. However, the TAWP's very simplicity makes it Republican kryptonite. Indeed, the Fox Propaganda network and right-wing podcasters would melt trying to tell their audiences why they *shouldn't* receive 'free' money.

This policy would decimate the GOP. Capitol Hill will need an Amazon-style painkiller dispensing machine to hand out all that Advil to the self-serving GOP hacks who masquerade as politicians.

But perhaps a headache would be the least of their problems when set alongside a much more sinister fate. Consider how GOP reps feared their voters attacking them during the meaningless House Speaker race of 2023[370]. Now imagine how terrified they will be if they try to stop those same AR-15-owning red state voters from getting their $2500 'entitlement.'

This being so, come 2028, Republicans will probably have neatly gerrymandered the big cities in the swing states to dilute their votes. There's nothing Democrats can do to stop this. However, the 229 million people eligible to receive the TAWP aren't just in the cities and the suburbs; they are in hitherto unwinnable Democratic target areas like rural Georgia, Florida, and Texas.

Of course, you want to know how the hell we are going to fund this $572 billion plan? In Chapter Eighteen, you will see not only how this is paid for but also how the TAWP acts as a magic key to unlock the door to everything else Democrats dream about, like Medicare for All, paid family leave, and paid sick leave.

Imagine if smart, progressive Democrats took this idea and ran with it in 2028. I'm a realist rather than an idealist, so I know that 155 million extra people won't vote Democratic. However, we only need ten million non-voters or GOP voters who want the TAWP to come over to the Democratic side to effect a landslide.

Just to segue to the point of money in politics and campaign finance reform. You may know about the 2012 Citizens United ruling handed down at the Supreme Court that allowed corporations and billionaires to make near-unlimited campaign donations in order to buy elections[371]. Indeed, in the 2024 election, the fragile, friendless freak, Mad Musk, pumped Trump full of nearly $300 million in donations and also set up a fraudulent lottery to snare new voters[372]. Not to be left out, billionaire-at-birth nepo-baby Timothy Mellon bestowed $125 million on Trump[373]. They were just two among many bawling billionaire bullies all in for authoritarianism[374].

So it is that Democrats also need to depend on ultra-rich, but more socially liberal donors—who are fairly content with the economic system just the way it is—to raise the billions of dollars to fight that far-right-funded propaganda[375]. Suffice to say, in Democratic primary elections, those donors always back status quo politicians; the same 'moderates' who never push for popular policies like universal healthcare, a $15 minimum wage, paid family leave, or paid sick leave. But here's the thing. When you have millions of energetic, inspired new voters, you don't need rich donors (or their political lapdogs) because you don't need to pay for the expensive television adverts to fight the far-right's BS. The TAWP is the advertisement that everyone will be talking about, and when you read about how we pay for it, you'll see that we've only just begun.

Chapter 16

The Small Oasis Of Social Democracy In America

Imagine an America where, without a college degree, you could get a job that pays at least $15 an hour, gives subsidized childcare, subsidized food, subsidized housing, free healthcare, free sick leave, free college tuition, and a good pension[376].

In this multiracial wonderland, your children and loved ones can grow up in a safe environment, without guns, without school shootings, and with next to no crime. Also, for kids, this paradise will provide schools that are citadels of facts, logic, reason, and evidence. Suffice to say, in this dreamlike America, women are free to choose what happens to their own bodies.

If you like the sound of all that, you'll be happy to learn that it exists today in an organization with a $900 billion turnover. Perhaps it's Apple? or Amazon? or Google? Nope. This paragon of social democratic values—even more generous than most Scandinavian countries—comes courtesy of your very own federal government in the form of the United States Military.

This should be a dream for Democrats to talk about. Yet, most Americans are completely unaware that the military is a place where almost every current 'divisive' national issue has been resolved; whether it's the minimum wage, childcare, healthcare, education, diversity, equal rights, or gun control.

Of course, you want receipts. No worries. You may recall Professor-turned-police-officer Rosa Brooks from the chapter "How to Make Cops Love Liberals." Well, brilliant people don't stand still. So it was, back in the Obama administration, she was a high-ranking DOD official whose expertise was further informed by her being married to a soldier.

As fortune would have it, Professor Brooks wrote a magnificent study of the military in her 2017 book, "How Everything Became War and the Military Became Everything." In one section, she described the life;

> Members of the military and their families can also lay claim to some of America's most generous social programs. The military offers free health care to service members and their dependents, discount groceries, tax-free shopping, subsidized child care, tuition assistance that can be transferred to spouses and children, and a host of other services. This creates numerous strange ironies: even as the post–New Deal welfare state continues its slow collapse; the military has become a substitute welfare state for a large swath of small-town America. In a sense, the military—despite its reputation for political conservatism—has become the last outpost of Big Government paternalism in the United States.[377]

Whichever branch you choose, whether you are a Marine Corps combat correspondent, as Vice President J.D. Vance was, or an elite Army Ranger, as Democratic congressional representative Jason Crow was,[378] you will always start on a living wage. As an E1 Private, entry-level pay begins at $24,000, plus all the benefits like healthcare, housing, and free education[379]. The military also offers the largest program of childcare in America, costing families just $200 per month[380].

Appearing in 2022 on combat veteran Ken Harbaugh's outstanding 'Burn the Boats' podcast, Army veteran Josh Remillard, running for Congress in North Carolina in the 2022 midterms, said;

> As far as medical care for you and your family are concerned, bear in mind that in America, the biggest cause of bankruptcy is medical bills. Well, here the largest deductible is $100, and even for catastrophic care, the deductible is capped at only $1000. And that care goes on for the whole of your life.[381]

There's another mind-bending fact. Our friends at the New York Times reported in 2023 that there are 161 public schools run by the Department of Defense Education Activity (DoDEA).

In those schools, there are 8,000 teachers educating 66,000 children of military members and civilian employees. When tested for reading and math and measured against the federal gold standard of judging school districts, DoDEA-educated children outperform both other public schools and charter schools[382].

In the GOP's war on public education, Democrats never talk about these schools, even though they are a current reality rather than the wonkish fantasy of a think tank's 200-page position paper.

Bearing in mind the fifty-three million children in public schools, it's worth expanding on this, as these places are a dream list for perfect public schools.

First, they are well-funded. This means that there are no four-day school weeks here. Suffice to say, the teachers are also well paid.

Then, the schools are integrated, regardless of ethnicity, gender, religion, political affiliation, or socio-economic background.

Another very important facet for the 'woke' military is a belief in basic facts. In their schools, children are taught science, they are taught history, and they are taught to respect each other. So, they grow up learning that the Earth is thirteen billion years old, climate change is real, and slavery actually happened.

Something else that might also amaze liberals. These schools have no elected school boards. This means there are no demented hags from 'Moms for Liberty' banning books and screaming that teachers are "groomers." Nor are there any Proud Boys waiting outside the school gates to really groom the kids.

To see the inclusive wonder of military life opens the window on why the far-right tries to conflate the term 'woke' with the term 'weak' when they talk about the military. This is odd because when I see progressive vets like Pete Buttigieg, Jason Crow, Ruben Gallego, Allison Gill, Lucas Kunce, Wes Moore, or Richard Ojeda, 'weak' is the last thing on my mind.

To explain, recall that, for the far-right, every accusation is an admission; thus, anything that doesn't center the John Wayne-style, straight, white, male patriarch—and relegate people of color, women, and LGBTQ+ folks to menial roles, or, even better, invisibility—must be bad. So it is that they hate the 'woke' military for showing heroic, white, black and brown, men and women working together to help keep America strong.

Just as an aside, that word 'woke' will invariably come from the mouth of a fragile, never-served, whiny weakling like Tucker Carlson, Charlie Kirk, or Matt Walsh. What a soldier might teach these cowards is this: in a firefight, no one cares what you look like, who you love, or who you pray to. What they do care about is that, when the squad SAW gunner gets hit, you can drag them to safety, pick up their M249, lay down covering fire, and on reload, know whether the weapon is fed by a belt of 7.62 x 51 mm or 5.56 x 45 mm ammo[383].

On the subject of guns, there's something that regular Americans may fall off their stools at hearing. Despite bases being crammed full of weapons-proficient, testosterone-fueled young men, there are no shootings. Of course, this might have something to do with the fact that, on the base, gun safety is paramount and all weapons are stored safely in the armory[384].

To conclude. Knowing all that you have read in just over a thousand words, how, in the name of everything that is good and proper, are Democrats so completely incapable of pointing out the obvious? The way the military looks after their own is a blueprint for a life that every American deserves.

Chapter 17

How To Go To Harvard University For $12,000 A Year.

Why shouldn't every clever student, regardless of household income, be able to go to Harvard? Shouldn't true meritocracy allow every young person the opportunity to travel as far as their talents allow?

That means the best and the brightest receiving the best education, all in the service of keeping America on top of the world. Keep reading, and by the end of this chapter, you will see how a student could go to Harvard for just $12,000 a year.

Every year, the top third of the brightest students leave high school to go on to the six thousand universities or colleges across the nation. That's eighteen million students[385].

I'll bet, though, for most people, all they know of higher education is of pupils going into debt to finance their education and of the far-right crying about 'free speech'—whilst simultaneously demanding action be taken against peaceful campus protesters. I can only offer a solution to solve the first of those issues.

So it is that we need to talk about the quality of education in a standard four-year degree. According to US News and World Report rankings, the top sixty institutions all have a graduation rate of 85%. The next 250 colleges (still the upper 5%) have graduation rates of above 70%. Yet, shockingly, nearly 90% (5,200) of higher-learning institutions have below 50% graduation rates[386].

Just to pick out a couple of examples, let's go to Utah State University. Fees are $13,000 a year, but graduation rates are only 49%. Or there's the University of West Georgia. Here, annual tuition is $16,000, but graduation rates are just 39%[387].

Never to disparage these places, but if you're going to be saddled with college debt, perhaps you should expect a better than 39% chance of graduating. After all, the primary purpose of college or university is to provide you with an education that will allow you to reach the promise of your talents.

It can't go unremarked that many of the low graduation-rate institutions have no incentive to change; after all, the pupils represent a guaranteed source of income for their businesses.

Despite this, if we want the best for all Americans, we need to show that we have their backs and that we care. To that point, I have an idea that can give pupils who go to institutions like Utah State or UWG the best value for their money, a far better chance of graduating, and the possibility of a much brighter career. To understand how, we must visit an altogether different world.

Most of the people we hear from in politics, business, and science have graduated from the eight elite 'Ivy League' institutions. These are Brown, Columbia, Cornell, Dartmouth, Harvard, Princeton, the University of Pennsylvania, and Yale. Combined, they educate 160,000 students. If we include the Massachusetts Institute of Technology (MIT), Caltech, Carnegie Mellon, and Stanford, we've added in another 45,000 students. However, even then, they only teach 1% of all pupils.

Those lucky enough to be educated at an Ivy were most probably born into a wealthy family with great connections. Just to note, a four-year degree at Harvard would set you back $330,000[388].

Or you may be one of a handful of really clever regular pupils who receive a scholarship and enough of a grant to afford accommodation, books, and food. Either way, you're motivated, your fellow students are motivated, and the faculty are motivated. Graduation rates at Princeton and Harvard are 87%.

Then, factor in that every employer knows that your degree is the gold standard and an absolute guarantee of excellence. Thus, when you graduate, there will be a great job and a top salary waiting for you. From this, you can see why the graduation rates are so high.

At this point, we need to take a small but relevant detour. Harvard, with its 21,000 pupils, has an endowment, which is a fund of donations. It totals over $50 billion. It's said, not unironically, that Harvard is an endowment with a university attached to it, and the purpose of the university is to educate a handful of rich kids, many of whose parents have donated a lot of cash to Harvard and who themselves may donate even more.

Princeton is even more exclusive, with only 8,500 students and $38 billion in the bank. The mistresses of Wall Street ensure that their endowment returns $4 billion, compared with operating costs of only $1.8 billion[389]. In fact, in 2023, the top ten wealthiest universities in America had nearly $300 billion in the bank[390].

You may wonder how those endowments got so large. Well, very rich alumni give enormous sums. Like Trump supporter John Paulson. This character manages a Wall Street hedge fund. That is a pool of rich people's money that gambles on the stock market. Paulson is big on Trump, which implies he's not so big on paying the taxes that would help Americans[391]. Nonetheless, he was happy to donate $400 million to Harvard in 2015[392].

In another case, another billionaire Trump-supporting hedge fund owner, Ken Griffin, has so much cash, he's donated $500 million to top up Harvard's already overflowing coffers[393].

One minor point, gentle reader. These donations are a tax write-off, so effectively, you, the taxpayers, must carry the burden of the hundreds of millions of dollars in federal taxes that John and Ken *didn't* have to pay[394].

For some of the rich, their donations are a quid pro quo for their kids being admitted. Then, those same rich folks' kids come out with their Ivy

League degrees. They may get a job on Wall Street or in the corporate media, or perhaps working at the DSCC, admonishing progressive politicians for actually speaking out about the issues that affect working people. All the while, they are blissfully oblivious to the fact that the donations their parents paid got them into Harvard in the first place.

But you're reading this chapter because you want to know how a regular smart kid can go to one of these elite institutions for just $12,000. Could it be by expanding the Ivy League's intake?

Harvard has 21,000 students, whereas in Canada, the elite University of Toronto teaches 61,700. Princeton teaches 8,500, while the excellent Canadian McGill University educates 37,000, and Yale educates 14,000 pupils, far less than the outstanding University of British Columbia, which teaches 71,000[395].

Even if it were possible to double the size of the Ivies and the other fifty universities that make up the top 1%, they would still only take in around an extra million students, which hardly scratches the surface of the problem.

We need to dream on a much bigger canvas to hope to effect the truly radical change that would benefit the millions of students currently being failed. As we have established, we can't send millions of these bright boys and girls from Maine, Michigan, and Missouri to universities like Yale or MIT because they simply don't have the space.

So instead, we bring Harvard, MIT, and Stanford to their states. What I envision is allowing some colleges with under 50% graduation rates to become satellite colleges of Harvard, Cornell, Yale, MIT, or any of those other top sixty universities.

Think of it as spreading the elite magic. After all, what's the point of having some of the finest citadels of learning if everyone can't access them? Well, that is exactly the point, but that's a whole other philosophical discussion. Regardless, this is a win-win for all concerned. The failing colleges get kissed by the top 1% 'magic', and the elite universities can charge a franchise fee to the college or university.

This would be one of the fastest ways to give American students access to a brilliant education that they can be proud of. Imagine if ten million students were enrolled in satellite colleges of the top sixty universities, with the college paying a $3,000 a year 'franchise fee' to the university. So, for helping Americans get a much brighter future, those elite institutions would earn over $30 billion a year.

You may have your doubts that the elite institutions would want to share their magic. Well, we have offered the $30 billion carrot, but there's also a stick. If they don't want to play ball, then perhaps it's time to consider raising the tax rate on the $20 billion a year in profits they make on their endowments. Currently, they are set at 1.4%, but they could increase to 25%, or their charitable status could disappear altogether[396].

It might also have crossed the minds of the slightly more cynical that this could put the rich folks' noses out of joint by devaluing a 'real' Ivy League university degree. It's a fair point, but it also slightly misses the point. For elites, an Ivy League education is all about the *experience*.

Take Harvard, for instance. The children of the rich would still bask in the glorified magnificence of an institution dating all the way back to 1636. They would learn at a bastion of excellence that has produced one hundred and fifty Nobel laureates. They would walk the same halls, study in the same libraries, and eat at the same tables as eight former presidents, including John F. Kennedy, Franklin Roosevelt, George W. Bush, and Barack Obama[397].

Hold those thoughts whilst we travel to the University of West Georgia, where just 39% of students graduate, but 100% are saddled with over $48,000 of debt. Even if you graduate from there, realistically, when you turn up at a job interview with that degree, does it really have any merit?

Now, imagine if this university was a Harvard satellite. Think how motivated the students would be.

Once admitted, UWG pupils would learn in their own lecture halls, receiving on forty-foot screens real-time live feeds from Harvard lectures.

So, they would learn exactly the same material, from exactly the same tutors, at exactly the same time, and complete exactly the same exams, with exactly the same grading scale as Harvard pupils. At the end of their $48,000 course, they would get a degree that said 'HARVARD CAMPUS AT UNIVERSITY OF WEST GEORGIA.'

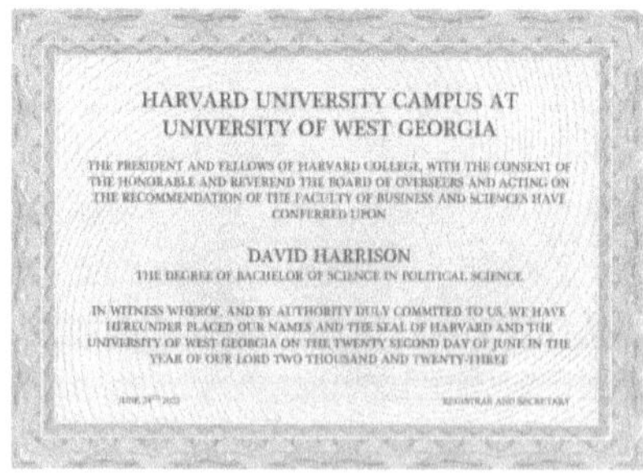

Now, when an employer sees this degree, it means something. This doesn't just work for science, business, or the humanities. It can be for engineering too. After all, think of all the rural solar, wind, and energy storage we're going to need, and all the trained engineers we are going to need to build it.

The best engineering universities in America are Harvard, MIT, and the University of California, Berkeley. Now, imagine a bright engineering student from anywhere in the nation being able to get a first-class education in their own state. Perhaps: "MIT CAMPUS AT UTAH STATE UNIVERSITY"

What you've just read is just another concrete way to show urban and rural working folks—both groups that are souring on the Democratic Party—that we care about their lives.

Chapter 18

Two Words to Terrify a Billionaire

In chapter fifteen, you read about the TAWP policy of $2500 annual payments to the 229 million Americans that would cost $572 billion and win over millions of new friends. You may want to know how all this largesse gets paid for.

Well, back in the year 2000, there was a candidate running for the presidency who proposed a 14.25% levy on people with assets of over $10 million. The candidate estimated it would raise $5.7 trillion. In his words;

> The plan I am proposing today does not involve smoke and mirrors, phony numbers, financial gimmicks, or the usual economic chicanery you usually find in Disneyland-on-the-Potomac. By my calculations, 1 percent of Americans, who control 90 percent of the wealth in this country, would be affected by my plan.[398]

It might seem funhouse-mirror absurd today, but that plan belonged to one Donald John Trump. It was the foundation of his economic argument as the candidate for the Reform Party.

It was probably a lie, but if not, it could have set him up as one of the greatest presidents of all time. Still, his loss is our gain. But, before we get to our plan, we need to talk about how we're drowning in debt.

A government can only spend what it receives in taxation. Any extra needs to come from borrowing. So it is that in 2024, Uncle Sam labors under the weight of $35 trillion of debt. Just the annual interest payments alone, at $870 billion, exceed the total defense budget [399].

This is one of the least talked about, yet most dire problems facing America today. Don't just take my word for it; let's hear from an authority: "The path we're on is unsustainable, and we'll have to get off that path sooner rather than later." That was Federal Reserve Chair Jerome Powell speaking in October 2023[400].

Accumulating more and more debt means that we face a trifecta of unpalatable options. Either we borrow more, make spending cuts, or raise taxes.

If we want to borrow more, our enormous debt and weak credit mean bond investors will demand higher interest rates. That will jack up the interest rates for regular people's car loans, home loans, and student loans. Cue angry voters.

Our second option is to cut spending on social programs and infrastructure. Down that road, society crumbles, which also ensures many angry voters.

Which leaves us with the third option: tax rises. I struggle to think of a faster way to lose an election.

To illustrate the debt conundrum, we just have to look at the federal budget. In 2024, the government spent $6.7 trillion, but it only received $4.9 trillion in taxes. This is how we get the federal deficit. In 2024, it was $1.8 trillion[401].

The reason we are in such massive debt is Sesame Street simple: we don't collect enough taxes from the corporations or the wealthy. Just to explain, today, the highest rate of tax on earnings above $570,000 is just 37%[402].

Yet, under FDR in 1942, the highest marginal rate of tax for rich folks was 88% on earnings over $200,000 ($3.6 million in 2024 money.)[403]. At the end of the war, Harry Truman raised them to 94% on all income over

$200,000. During MAGA's fabled 1950s, Dwight Eisenhower, the last decent and effective Republican president, kept taxes at 92% on all earnings above $400,000[404].

I can hear my libertarian friends wailing about high taxes stifling innovation and growth, so let's address that. First, though, I need to separate income from corporate taxes. From the 1950s to the 1980s, corporation taxes were around 50%, and there were no loopholes[405]. Yet, today, even though the tax rate for large corporations is only 21%, many firms pay next to nothing. In 2021, Ford paid 1%, Exxon Mobil paid 2.8%, Merck paid 4%, and Amazon and Nike paid around 6%[406]. Some of this is explained by the 80% of the pre-tax profits of the S&P 500 (large corporations) no longer used in research and development or capital investment but in buying back their own stock. This legal scam decreases the stock in the market and boosts the stock price, to which the CEOs and board members' pay and compensation are linked. It's also helpful for these giant corporations that stock buybacks are only taxed at 1%[407].

Going back to the post-war years. Even with 50% corporation taxes and 90% income taxes, businesses made good profits, and, oddly enough, all the rich folks all stayed in America. Take bankers as an example. From the 1950s to the late 1970s, long before they were the 'Mistresses of Wall Street,' they had the 3-6-3 rule[408]: they borrowed at 3%, lent at 6%, and were on the golf course by 3 PM.

As for American innovation. In 1954, Bell Laboratories built the first solar panels that would power satellites in space. Ford built the GT40 to take on Ferrari at Le Mans in 1964. In 1969, Boeing put the 747 jetliner into service, and the first F-14 Tomcat—the same plane as Tom Cruise flew in Top Gun—was built in 1970.

Then there are some of the astonishing inventions that we got before the 1980s: the calculator, the digital watch, the microwave, the Sony Walkman, the Kodak instant camera, the Xerox machine, the catalytic convertor, the personal computer, the mobile phone, the television, the AR-15, Kevlar,

X-ray machines, MRI machines, the Abrams tank, the Internet, GPS, wind power, and hydropower.

All this gives lie to the BS that innovation dries up when taxes are high. I know you're skeptical, so I'm providing a receipt from a man who's worth $159 billion[409]. Bill Gates started Microsoft in 1975, when the tax rate for top earners was 70%[410]. When asked about those taxes, Gates replied,

> In the 1970s, when Paul Allen and I were starting Microsoft, marginal tax rates were almost twice the top rate today. It didn't hurt our incentive to build a great company."..."Americans in the top 1% can afford to pay a lot more, before they stop going to work or creating jobs.[411]

Back in 2019, a Fox News poll showed nearly three-quarters of Americans surveyed favored raising taxes on people earning over $10 million a year to fund spending. Indeed, over two-thirds of respondents even wanted them raised on those earning $1 million[412].

So, here's the question. If Fox News viewers want higher taxes on the rich, and so do progressive Democrats, why can't they sync together? The answer is straightforward. Because, to neuter the idea, the GOP and their right-wing shills just scream 'Socialism!' and dream up another crap story or three-letter bullshit acronym to terrify and enrage their low-information voters. This has the effect of making those voters mad about DEI, Hunter Biden's laptop, or Haitians 'eating' pets. All great GOP misdirection to ensure they never look up to see who's really screwing them over.

We have spoken about the TAWP. With that, a lot of that right-wing BS falls away. But there's more good stuff coming that will bury the Ayn Rand nonsense forever.

Before that, we need to know who needs to pay. According to the Federal Reserve, in 2024, the richest 1% of Americans—those with over

$11 million in assets—control over $44 trillion in wealth[413]. That's 1% controlling nearly the same as the other 90% of lower and middle-income citizens *combined.* Just to paint a picture, the richest 1% comprises only 2.3 million people, yet they have more wealth than the 238 million Americans who make up the lower 90%[414].

Let's just get those 2.3 million people in perspective. Two million of them have between $11 million and $30 million in wealth.

Moving up the wealth ladder. There are 208,000 people with over $30 million in wealth. These are the richest 0.1% of Americans. Wealth managers call these UHNWI—Ultra high net worth individuals—and in 2024 they have combined assets of $24 trillion[415].

At the apex, we come to the 0.01%. We know about Bezos, Musk, and Zuckerberg, but there are 832 other billionaires, almost all of whom have become so since 1980[416]. The combined wealth of those 835 individuals in 2024 is $5.8 trillion[417]. If they were a nation, they would be the third-largest economy on the planet, after the US and China[418].

Democrats have made proposals, yet little ever happens because it's 'anti-American' to tax the 'makers.' Also, without the shield of the TAWP, most voters aren't energized to press for the tax rises. Still, some Dems have suggested 70% taxes on earnings above $10 million. I have no objection to this, but I can show why it won't raise much in practice. Allow me to introduce you to the deliberately opaque-sounding 'Securities Backed Line of Credit' (SBLOC). It's more aptly styled *"Buy, Borrow, Die"* and was dreamed up by some evil genius to allow the modern-day robber barons to take out a loan backed by their assets. Then, because loans are tax free, they never count as income, so the borrower pays no income tax, capital gains tax, or estate taxes[419].

Like the year 2000 Trump, I want a wealth tax because I know what these rich characters can never move is their wealth. It's their wealth in stocks, bonds, art, land, and property that they use as collateral for those tax-free loans. The wealth is always there, somewhere.

If we take Mad Musk. As of December 2024, he was worth $400 billion, most of it in stock from Tesla and SpaceX[420]. He could try to hide it, but even if he gave his stock to his kids, it's still there, easily traceable and easily valued.

The same goes for the ultra-rich, who own those mansions, mega-yachts, and Monet paintings.

Thus, to pay for the TAWP and make life better for 90% of regular Americans, I propose the PABEF ACT: "PROVIDING AMERICANS A BETTER FUTURE." It's a graduated annual wealth tax on the richest 1% of Americans. Those rich folks with between $11 and $30 million of assets will pay 10%. For the super-rich, with wealth between $30 million and $1 billion, it's 15%, and for the insanely rich who have fortunes above $1 billion, it's 20% [421].

At this point, you're probably thinking that Sadistic Sam, Corrupt Clarence, and Know-Nothing Neil, sitting high in the Supreme Court, will immediately strike this down. However, recall that to get this far, we had to give two hundred and thirty million Americans the TAWP. So, those people love the government and will never want their entitlements taken away. This means they will be happy to tax the rich to pay for it.

So, for the GOP activists masquerading as Supreme Court justices, to stop the wealth tax, it's a FAFO moment where America would get to see the same fools who legalized machine guns trying to withhold an entitlement from the people who own those machine guns.

Leaving the drama of that potential excitement aside, there is another argument that I can bring in favor of the wealth tax on unrealized assets that should see it sail through. A precedent already exists without which many state budgets would collapse. Let me allow Senator Elizabeth Warren to give you the punchline;

> You've been paying a wealth tax for years. They just call it a property tax. I just want their tax to include the diamonds, the yachts, and the Rembrandts.[422]

Senator Warren is exactly right. If you pay property taxes, you're paying a wealth tax, assessed on the value of your largest unrealized asset, your home, a.k.a., your wealth. It may be 1.3% in Texas, or 0.8% in Kentucky, or 0.9% in Georgia, but everyone is liable.

Thus, when the corrupt, robed shills at the Supreme Court try to argue against the wealth tax, we put them in checkmate by showing that they are also arguing against every state collecting any property taxes. Cue GOP congressional reps, senators, state reps, and governors, all on the phone to the Court, imploring them not to collapse their tax base. That's how liberals should play the game: by forcing the hacks to make a real argument grounded in facts[423].

The PABEF tax could raise up to $6.1 trillion. When we add that to the $4.9 trillion that we currently collect from general taxation, we are up to $10.7 trillion. The richest 1% will squeal, but no one will be listening.

Now we have options. The $6.7 trillion federal budget will be balanced. That means that we can start paying off the $35 trillion national debt by $1 trillion a year. Then, deduct the $572 billion cost of the TAWP, and we still have $2.4 trillion left. This is where we can help the nearly two-thirds of Americans living paycheck to paycheck[424].

With the GOP punch-drunk, we can bring in the progressive policies that can make most people's lives better:

- FREE HEALTHCARE - MEDICARE FOR ALL AMERI-

CANS

- THREE MONTHS PAID FAMILY LEAVE.

- THREE MONTHS PAID SICK LEAVE.

- FREE PRE-K.

- FREE CHILD CARE FOR HOUSEHOLDS WITH UNDER $75000 INCOME

- CHILD CARE FOR HOUSEHOLDS WITH $75-100K HOUSEHOLD INCOME = JUST $2000 A YEAR.

- FREE SCHOOL MEALS.

- MEDICARE PRESCRIPTION COSTS NEVER TO GO ABOVE $2000.

Apart from Medicare for All, all these fabulous proposals were in the $3 trillion, 2468-page Build Back Better plan that Senators Joe Manchin and Kyrsten Sinema killed in 2022. We can and should rail against them, but the truth is the administration did a terrible job of messaging such wonderful policies. Once again, the Democrats were speaking 'wonkish,' a language only they understand.

There are two aspects to great messaging. First, make a complicated idea simple, and then they repeat that idea again and again because great ideas never get boring. To the first point, just look at how easy it was to explain the Build Back Better plan. A mere fifty words on eight lines show how we can immeasurably improve the lives of Americans.

You don't have to be a Nobel Prize-winning economist to understand that these policies could make a family of three with $60,000 of annual household income up to $16,000 better off ($11k childcare, $5k TAWP payments). And there's no need to be a genius political strategist to figure out how this may energize voters. As for the cost of those programs, excluding healthcare, it was just $531 billion[425].

We still have $1.9 trillion left over. This will be used for the big one: Medicare for All.

This has other names, such as National Health Service, Universal Healthcare, or Single Payer Healthcare. Regardless, according to the Kaiser Family Foundation, nearly half of American adults say they struggle with their monthly health insurance premiums. It's hardly surprising when the average cost of single coverage is about $8500 a year, and a family plan comes in at a wallet-busting $23,000[426].

One of the great myths Democrats have never fought back against is that a switch to Medicare for All would bankrupt America. Conventional wisdom says that we would need a magic money tree to pay for it all. Not true.

An astonishing fact that liberals never mention is that the government already spends $1.8 trillion on healthcare. Then, factor in the $560 billion on government-funded third-party programs, and we hit $2.3 trillion[427]. To break it down. Uncle Sam, a.k.a. 'The Government,' is currently paying for the eighty-seven million people covered by Medicaid and CHIP (children's healthcare)[428]. Then, Medicare protects another sixty-five million seniors[429]. Add in the nine million veterans covered by the Veterans Health Administration[430], and we are at 161 million Americans, or half the country, who already have a form of Medicare for All.

So, let's talk about the cost of this 'socialized' healthcare. The National Library of Medicine estimates the annual costs of Medicare for All at $3 trillion. Recall that we are already spending $2.3 trillion, so we add in another $700 billion, and the prize is ours[431]. For a second opinion, in February 2021, the Congressional Budget Office estimated the additional cost of universal healthcare. Their worst-case scenario set the cost at $696 billion[432].

With this combination of life-changing policies, suddenly, every American gets to see the government working for them.

Then, with the remaining $1.5 trillion, we can launch the Climate Rescue Corps to transition to clean, green, cheap energy, and rebuild our inner cities. All of which will provide millions of new jobs.

Everything that you've read about in this book shows you that self-interest is a massive motivator.

Go ask your MAGA uncle whether he'd rather be mad about DEI or have free healthcare and an extra $2500 a year in his pocket. I'll bet dollars to donuts his red cap would be in the trash.

That is how you win over millions of GOP voters and millions of non-voters and sweep places that were once unimaginable, like Florida, Missouri, Texas, and Tennessee.

Presumably, the Heritage Foundation will close for lack of business, and everyone will forget about MAGA and Donald J.....Who?

Without far-right obstruction, Americans will finally see that they don't have to bow down to the ultra-rich and corrupt corporations. This will open the door to fair taxation of corporations, income tax rises on those earning over one million dollars per year, and estate tax rises on those with estates of over $10 million. The US Treasury could also economically bludgeon the offshore tax havens that hide much of the wealthy's money, like the Bahamas and the Cayman Islands, into submission.

But there's more. This renewed American leadership will be a pathfinder for the world, showing other nations how to banish the scourge of right-wing billionaire-funded, Robin Hood-in-reverse, fake 'populism'—which always punches down at the marginalized to provide cover for the ultra-rich to keep stealing all the money—and help these societies rebuild their middle classes for a truly hopeful future.

Chapter 19

Something Else You May Enjoy Reading.

I f you liked this book, you may enjoy another title of mine, The Confederate Taliban. Here's the opening chapter.

MAKE AMERICA GREAT AGAIN. MAKE AMERICA STRAIGHT AGAIN. MAKE AMERICA WHITE AGAIN. MAKE AMERICA RIGHT AGAIN.

While debating hatred is a fool's errand, arguing with ignorance can prove a more fruitful undertaking, so here's a retort to the first words of this chapter.

"So If it's the blacks, browns, LGBTQ+, Jews, and woke liberals causing all your problems, please explain something to me. Starting in the 1600s, early settlers, possibly including your forebears, came over from Europe into a 'whites only' America. The slave colony in the south would have been of no concern to them unless they were benefiting from it. Then, for the next two hundred and fifty years, America was wide open and free for the taking, with the only competition coming from other straight, white, Anglo-Saxon folks.

By the 1860s, across the West, the United States Army had kindly wiped out most of the pesky brown people—whose civilization was here first—in order to steal their land. Had your relatives traveled there, Uncle Sam would have gifted them one hundred and sixty acres of that land that would be worth over two million dollars today.

The even more adventurous among your kin could have headed to California to strike gold. Or, if 'black gold' was their thing, they could have scooped up scrubland in Texas to become oil barons. Always remember, throughout this time, straight, white men reigned supreme, with no black, brown, Jewish, or LGBTQ+ folks allowed to compete with your great-grandparents.

But, perhaps your forefathers came here too late to take advantage of all the free land and gold? No problem. During the boom years following the end of the Second World War, they could have started any business and cleaned up, almost completely untroubled by challenges from marginalized groups.

"So, given all these infinite possibilities and endless opportunities for creating generational wealth, what the hell were your people doing back then that you're not a multimillionaire today?"

Maybe some of the other side genuinely don't know, or maybe they do. Someone less kind-hearted might use the same line conservatives use on poor black folks; that their ancestors were too lazy or too weak to succeed. But I'm not that person, and this is not one of those books.

I understand that the system is functioning exactly as planned and that the outcomes are precisely as intended. That system, which secured the votes of working-and lower-middle class white folks, was never intended to educate them, nor were their ancestors ever meant to ascend to positions of influence, wealth, or power.

Instead, they were the indentured servants in the 1700s, deceived by their bosses and denied their promised hundred acres after fulfilling their obligations. They were the coal miners in the 1900s, striking for their rights, whose bosses ordered them beaten by the Pinkertons and shot by the police. They were the soldiers sent off to war, while the bosses' kids stayed home. Then, coming home, shattered from the horrors of seeing things no human should ever see and from doing things no human should ever do, they found themselves thrown away.

This is the design because this is who they always were: the disposable, the malleable, and the replaceable, but allowed the slight advantage of standing one rung on the ladder above other folks.

In 1865, 1954, 1964, 2008, and 2020, Americans may have thought they had overcome hate and division. However, many never saw the demonic force, once beaten—but whose ideas were never vanquished and therefore never vanished—feeding and stoking the fires of fury.

What you may know as MAGA, I call the Confederate Taliban. They are the gun-wielding, freedom-hating, race-baiting, Russia-loving, women-hating, planet-heating Americans. They exist within a coalition of Scared, (fake) Christian, Angry, Rich and Insane (SCARI) people. In them, we find an unyielding need to subdue, dominate, and control anyone who will not conform to their dogma. Theirs is a world where they demand the right to do anything without having to take responsibility for anything they do.

That being said, it was F. Scott Fitzgerald, borrowing from the ancient Greek philosopher Aristotle, who wrote;

> The test of a first-rate intelligence is the ability to hold two opposing ideas in the mind at the same time and still retain the ability to function.

To prove the point, what has happened in America over the past four hundred years would be amazing if it were a country in Europe. But this is a country younger than some European homes.

America is the first nation to have institutionalized slavery and fought a civil war to end it. It's the first nation to create a legal apartheid state within its borders and then peacefully dismantle it, and it's the only nation whose citizens have walked on another planet.

As far as people go, it's the nation that gave us Robert Edward Lee and Frederick Douglass, Donald Trump and Dr. Martin Luther King Jr., and Phyllis Schlafly and Harriet Tubman. In a nutshell, America is the most exciting, diverse, and powerful society that humanity has ever produced.

If there is a single focus of light that could illuminate what an American can be, it is the ability of someone to dream the impossible and turn it into the possible, regardless of where they come from, what they look like, or who their parents are.

Maybe that's what a kid from Wapakoneta, Ohio, thought when, just thirty-nine years into his life, he became the first human to set foot on another planet. Conceivably, it may also have been in the mind of the skinny son of a single mom from Honolulu, who, forty-seven years into his time here on Earth, would become the 44th President of the United States.

The progress we have made should be an immense source of pride. America has evolved from a place where, just ninety-nine years ago, President Woodrow Wilson was screening the KKK promo video, "Birth of a Nation," in the White House. Yet, showing how two things can be true at once, Wilson's own grandson marched for civil rights and was proud to still be alive to see a black man stand for president?

Nevertheless, as we progress, we challenge interests that are adept at stoking fear in order to preserve their power. That can lead to regress; thus, Trump followed both Obama and Biden. Still, despite huge headwinds from the Confederate Taliban, this nation of over three hundred million people is moving relatively peacefully from a majority European ethnic culture to a majority non-European American culture, with white, black, and brown people learning together, working together, loving together, and living together.

Through the chapters, I hope to take you on an incredible journey. There are four recurring themes that will come up again and again, even though I won't specifically reference them: Self-interest, status, class, and race. It is impossible to understand America's past, present, or future without understanding these four characteristics. There's a fifth theme called 'courage'. Sometimes, I may point it out, but if you're reading this, you'll be smart enough to recognize it.

There are enough explanations and solutions within the chapters—not just from me, but, more importantly, from many other brilliant people—that by the end of the book, you will be energized to fight the fear and help build an astonishing American future.

Chapter 20

Acknowledgements and Reading/Listening List

Writing a book is a long and sometimes frustrating process. So, I have to thank my brother Ed for reading through it and offering some constructive criticism and praise. Also, my friend John and his brother, Andrew, who were kind enough to read early drafts and say they enjoyed it. Thanks also to my friend Stuart, who listened to me ramble on during our morning dog walks. I can't leave out my now-passed Dad, and still-here Mom. Without them and all the experiences they gave me, this never would have happened.

For the research, here are some of the books that helped light up my mind.

<u>Book Reading List:</u>
The Sum of Us by Heather McGhee.
Merge Left - Ian Haney Lopez
The Fifth Risk by Michael Lewis
The Liberal Redneck Manifesto by Trae Crowder
Evil Geniuses_ The Unmaking of America_ A Recent History by Kurt Andersen
Listen Liberal: Thomas Frank
Arguing with Zombies by Paul Krugman
How To Win Friends and Influence People by Dale Carnegie

1. https://www.nytimes.com/interactive/2024/11/05/us/elections/results-president.html

2. Dorman, J. L. (2024, November 12). AOC asked voters why they backed her candidacy and Trump's reelection. Instagram users pointed to the economy and Gaza. Business Insider. https://www.businessinsider.com/aoc-trump-harris-democrats-economy-gaza-split-ticket-voters-2024-11

3. " *Biden Caught on Hot Mic: "No one f—s with a Biden."* The Associated Press, 2022, https://www.youtube.com/watch?v=Mpk210Ee1Sg

4. Yang, Z. (2024, October 16). The Biden-Harris Macroeconomic Record Is Getting a Bum Rap. American Enterprise Institute - AEI. https://www.aei.org/economics/the-biden-harris-macroeconomic-record-is-getting-a-bum-rap/

5. Lane, S. (2023, December 25). The Hill. *The Hill.* https://thehill.com/homenews/administration/4375922-biden-rips-media-for-economy-coverage-start-reporting-it-the-right-way/

6. Luhby, T., & Davis, E. (2024, October 8). Harris proposes Medicare pay for home health care for first time. CNN. https://edition.cnn.com/2024/10/08/politics/harris-home-health-care-medicare-proposal

7. Geevarghese, J. (2024, November 14). Now is the time for finger-pointing. Democratic elites must own their loss. The Hill. https://thehill.com/opinion/campaign/4988643-democratic-party-challenge-harrison/

8. "Everyone is taking their skim": How Democratic consultants cashed in on Harris' losing campaign. (2024, November 24). Salon. https://www.salon.com/2024/11/24/everyone-is-taking-their-skim-how-democratic-consultants-cashed-in-on-harris-losing-campaign/

9. Farivar, M. (2024, November 7). In historic shift, American Muslim and Arab voters desert Democrats. Voice of America. https://www.voanews.com/a/in-historic-shift-american-muslim-and-arab-voters-desert-democrats/7854995.html

10. Gerbaud, G., Harrison, C., & Robertson, K. (2024, November 6). How Latinos Voted the 2024 U.S. Presidential Election. AS/COA. https://www.as-coa.org/articles/how-latinos-voted-2024-us-presidential-election

11. Trump and Musk discussed firing striking workers. The UAW is now seeking an NLRB investigation. (2024, August 13). PBS News. https://www.pbs.org/newshour/politics/trump-and-musk-discussed-firing-striking-workers-the-uaw-is-now-seeking-an-nlrb-investigation

12. Young voters shifted toward Trump but still favored Harris overall. (2024, November 12). Tufts Now. https://now.tufts.edu/2024/11/12/young-voters-shifted-toward-trump-still-favored-harris-overall

13. Thompson, S. (2024, December 8). 2024 Election Donald Trump voter regrets stories. BuzzFeed. https://www.buzzfeed.com/sarathompson1/donald-trump-voters-regrets-flipped

14. Leopards Eating People's Faces Party - Wiktionary, the free dictionary. (2022). Wiktionary. https://en.wiktionary.org/wiki/Leopards_Eating_People%27s_Faces_Party

15. https://link.motherjones.com/public/36678690

16. Schmidt, E. (2022). Reading the numbers: 130 million american adults have low literacy skills. APM Research Lab; American Public Media. https://www.apmresearchlab.org/10x-adult-literacy

17. Svirnovskiy, G. (2021, June 7). Paid leave is incredibly popular — even with Republicans. *Vox.* https://www.vox.com/2021/6/7/22380427/poll-paid-leave-popular-democrats-republicans-covid-19

18. Schaeffer, K. (2024, April 14). Most Americans support a $15 federal minimum wage. Pew Research Center. https://www.pewresearch.org/short-reads/2021/04/22/most-americans-support-a-15-federal-minimum-wage/

19. Brenan, B. M. (2024, February 7). Majority in U.S. still say gov't should ensure healthcare. *Gallup.com.* https://news.gallup.com/poll/468401/majority-say-gov-ensure-healthcare.aspx

20. Illing, S. (2023, April 16). Katie Porter thinks Democrats have a confidence problem. Vox. https://www.vox.com/the-gray-area/2023/4/16/23680245/katie-porter-democrats-confidence

21. Perkins, T. (2022, April 29). Revealed: top US corporations raising prices on Americans even as profits surge. The Guardian. https://www.theguardian.com/business/2022/apr/27/inflation-corporate-america-increased-prices-profits

22. Bloomberg - Are you a robot? (2024, March 7). Www.bloomberg.com. https://www.bloomberg.com/graphics/2024-opinion-biden-accomplishment-data/

23. Inc, G. (2021, October 6). GOP Now Viewed as Better Party for Security, Prosperity. Gallup.com. https://news.gallup.com/poll/355511/gop-viewed-better-party-security-prosperity.aspx

24. Bank of America Private Bank. (2022). *The impact of shifting generational attitudes amid an historic wealth transfer.* https://ustrustaem.fs.ml.com/content/dam/ust/articles/pdf/2022-BofaA-Private-Bank-Study-of-Wealthy-Americans.pdf

25. *Must-Know Inherited Wealth Statistics [Latest Report] • Gitnux.* (2023, December 16). GITNUX. https://gitnux.org/inherited-wealth-statistics/

26. Cohen, J. D. (n.d.). For A Dollar and A Dream: State Lotteries in Modern America. Next Big Idea Club. https://nextbigideaclub.com/magazine/dollar-dream-state-lotteries-modern-america-bookbite/36834/

27. Milman, O. (2014, February 6). Winning the lottery makes you more conservative, study finds. The Guardian; The Guardian. https://www.theguardian.com/money/2014/feb/06/winning-lottery-makes-you-more-conservative

28. Wikipedia contributors. (2024, March 27). *U.S. economic performance by presidential party*. Wikipedia. https://en.wikipedia.org/wiki/U.S._economic_performance_under_Democratic_and_Republican_presidents

29. The Editors of Encyclopaedia Britannica. (2024, October 16). 1983 Beirut barracks bombings | Summary, Casualties, & Lebanese Civil War. Encyclopedia Britannica. https://www.britannica.com/event/1983-Beirut-barracks-bombings

30. Zapata, C. (2023, November 16). United States invades Grenada. HISTORY. https://www.history.com/this-day-in-history/united-states-invades-grenada

31. Reuters. (2024, February 3). US troops in Middle East: What are they doing and where? *Voice of America*. https://www.voanews.com/a/us-troops-in-middle-east-what-are-they-doing-and-where-/7469452.html

32. Thiessen, M. A. (2023, December 1). Ukraine aid's best-kept secret: Most of the money stays in the U.S.A. *Washington Post*. https://www.washingtonpost.com/opinions/2023/11/29/ukraine-military-aid-american-economy-boost/

33. Digital, M. (n.d.). The Art of Public Speaking - Ethos3 - a presentation training and design agency. Ethos3 - a Presentation Training and Design Agency. https://ethos3.com/the-art-of-public-speaking/

34. Thakker, P. (2023, June 30). Republicans are taking credit for infrastructure bill they all voted against. The New Republic. https://newrepublic.com/post/173963/republicans-taking-credit-infrastructure-bill-voted-against

35. Drug companies cap prices of asthma inhalers. (2024, June 1). [Video]. NBC News. https://www.nbcnews.com/health/health-news/drugmakers-cap-cost-asthma-inhalers-35-month-rcna154536

36. https://www.fiercepharma.com/pharma/boehringer-ingelheim-slashes-out-pocket-inhaler-prices-35

37. Eidenmuller, M. E. (n.d.). *Jimmy Carter - A Crisis of Confidence Speech - American rhetoric*. https://www.americanrhetoric.com/speeches/jimmycartercrisisofconfidence.htm

38. Graefe, B. L. (n.d.). *Oil shock of 1978–79*. Federal Reserve History. https://www.federalrese rvehistory.org/essays/oil-shock-of-1978-79

39. https://www.walmart.com/browse/food/eggs/976759_9176907_1001469

40. *Car emissions & global warming*. (2014, July 18). Union of Concerned Scientists. https://w ww.ucsusa.org/resources/car-emissions-global-warming

41. Carrington, D. (2017, July 12). Want to fight climate change? Have fewer children. The Guardian; The Guardian. https://www.theguardian.com/environment/2017/jul/12/want -to-fight-climate-change-have-fewer-children

42. ElectricChoice.com. (2024, June 28). *Electricity Rates (Updated July 2024) — Electric Choice*. https://www.electricchoice.com/electricity-prices-by-state/

43. Dnistran, I. (2024, June 6). This Tesla Model S has 430,000 miles on the original battery and motors. InsideEVs. https://insideevs.com/news/722367/tesla-model-s-430000-miles-origin al-battery-motors/

44. The President's news conference. (n.d.). Ronald Reagan. https://www.reaganlibrary.gov/ar chives/speech/presidents-news-conference-23

45. *You tell 'em, Elizabeth Warren*. (2011, September 22). MSNBC.com. https://www.msnbc. com/the-last-word/you-told-em-elizabeth-warren-msna41789

46. Kates, J., Cox, C., & Michaud, J. (2023, March 10). *How much could COVID-19 vaccines cost the U.S. after commercialization? | KFF*. KFF. https://www.kff.org/coronavirus-covid-19/is sue-brief/how-much-could-covid-19-vaccines-cost-the-u-s-after-commercialization/

47. Health insurers are boosting CEO pay to astronomical heights while their customers suffer. (2023, June 20). https://jacobin.com/2023/06/health-insurance-ceo-pay-buybacks-taxpaye r-money

48. Sainato, M. (2016, February 10). A democracy lost to corporate socialism. The Hill. https://thehill.com/blogs/pundits-blog/economy-budget/268947-a-democracy-lost-t o-corporate-socialism/

49. Lalljee, J. (2022, January 17). Elon Musk is speaking out against government subsidies. Here's a list of the billions of dollars his businesses have received. *Business Insider*. https://www.busi nessinsider.com/elon-musk-list-government-subsidies-tesla-billions-spacex-solarcity-2021-12

50. Overly, S. (2021, December 5). This government loan program helped Tesla at a critical time. Trump wants to cut it. *Washington Post*. https://www.washingtonpost.com/news/innovations/wp/2017/03/16/this-governm ent-loan-program-helped-tesla-at-a-critical-time-trump-wants-to-cut-it/

51. Kharpal, A. (2021, May 18). What "regulatory credits" are — and why they're so important to Tesla. CNBC. https://www.cnbc.com/2021/05/18/tesla-electric-vehicle-regulatory-credits-explained.html

52. Domonoske, C. (2023, December 28). The $7,500 Tax Credit for Electric Cars Has Some Big Changes in 2024. What to Know. NPR. https://www.npr.org/2023/12/28/1219158071/ev-electric-vehicles-tax-credit-car-shopping-tesla-ford-vw-gm

53. Fridman, L. (2023, December 14). *Transcript for Jeff Bezos: Amazon and Blue Origin | Lex Fridman Podcast #405 - Lex Fridman*. Lex Fridman. https://lexfridman.com/jeff-bezos-transcript/

54. Statista. (2024, April 22). *Countries with the highest military spending 2023*. https://www.statista.com/statistics/262742/countries-with-the-highest-military-spending/

55. *President Dwight D. Eisenhower's Farewell Address (1961) | National Archives*. (n.d.). https://www.archives.gov/milestone-documents/president-dwight-d-eisenhowers-farewell-address

56. Defense Contractors Are Bilking the American People» Senator Bernie Sanders. (n.d.). Senator Bernie Sanders. https://www.sanders.senate.gov/op-eds/defense-contractors-are-bilking-the-american-people/

57. https://nffe.org/press-release/so-called-department-of-government-efficiency-would-be-responsible-for-nearly-500000-veteran-layoffs-if-musk-and-ramaswamy-execute-stated-plans/

58. Veterans and the Americans with Disabilities Act: A Guide for Employers. (2020, November 27). US EEOC. https://www.eeoc.gov/laws/guidance/veterans-and-americans-disabilities-act-guide-employers

59. Zaitchik, A. (2021, August 30). How the Bayh-Dole Act Wrested Public Science From the People's Hands. *The Intercept*. https://theintercept.com/2021/08/29/bayh-dole-act-public-science-patents/

60. *"Gaming" of U.S. patent system is keeping drug prices sky high, report says*. (2022, September 15). NBC News. https://www.nbcnews.com/health/health-news/gaming-us-patent-system-keeping-drug-prices-sky-high-report-says-rcna47507

61. Cleary, E. G., Cleary, Jackson, M. J., Ledley, F. D., & Center for Integration of Science and Industry. (2020). Government as the first investor in biopharmaceutical innovation: Evidence from new drug approvals 2010–2019. In Working Paper: Vol. No. 133. https://www.ineteconomics.org/uploads/papers/WP_133-Cleary-et-al-Govt-innovation.pdf

62. *Leading lobbying industries U.S. 2023 | Statista*. (2024, February 26). Statista. https://www.statista.com/statistics/257364/top-lobbying-industries-in-the-us/

63. Cubanski, J., Neuman, T., & Freed, M. (2024, March 6). *Explaining the prescription drug provisions in the Inflation Reduction Act | KFF*. KFF. https://www.kff.org/medicare/issue-brief/explaining-the-prescription-drug-provisions-in-the-inflation-reduction-act/

64. Cohen, J. P. (2024, March 12). Legal challenges to IRA drug price negotiations face skeptical judges. Forbes. https://www.forbes.com/sites/joshuacohen/2024/03/09/legal-challenges-to-ira-drug-price-negotiations-face-skeptical-judges/

65. Insider. (2019, January 28). 4 diseases that have been eliminated in the United States in the last 100 years. *Business Insider*. https://www.insider.com/diseases-eliminated-united-states-vaccines-2019-1

66. *The Virtue of Selfishness - AynRand.org*. (n.d.). AynRand.org. https://aynrand.org/novels/the-virtue-of-selfishness/

67. Hitchens, C. (2000, December 6). Greenspan shrugged. *Vanity Fair*. https://www.vanityfair.com/culture/2000/12/hitchens-200012

68. Clark, A., & Treanor, J. (2017, November 26). Greenspan - I was wrong about the economy. Sort of. *The Guardian*. https://www.theguardian.com/business/2008/oct/24/economics-creditcrunch-federal-reserve-greenspan

69. Kilgore, E. (2016, April 12). Donald Trump's role model is an Ayn Rand character. *Intelligencer*. https://nymag.com/intelligencer/2016/04/trumps-role-model-is-an-ayn-rand-character.html

70. https://twitter.com/stevanzetti/status/1650173018528792583

71. Williams, G. (2018, June 7). Silicon Valley's culture of breaking things is totally broken. *WIRED*. https://www.wired.com/story/move-fast-and-break-things-or-dont/

72. Ha, T. (2022, July 20). US Republican leaders love Ayn Rand's controversial philosophy—and are increasingly misinterpreting it. *Quartz*. https://qz.com/882493/donald-trump-paul-ryan-and-andy-puzder-say-they-love-ayn-rands-controversial-philosophy-heres-what-us-republicans-keep-getting-wrong-about-it

73. Emery, D. (2017, June 23). Did Ayn Rand receive social security benefits? Snopes. https://www.snopes.com/fact-check/ayn-rand-social-security/

74. Reich, Robert B., Saving Capitalism: For the Many, Not the Few. New York, Alfred A. Knopf, 2015.

75. James Truslow Adams and the Origins of "The American Dream" - Conversable Economist. (2019, July 4). Conversableeconomist.com. https://conversableeconomist.com/2019/07/04/james-truslow-adams-and-the-origins-of-the-american-dream/

76. Staff, H., & Staff, H. (2018, January 24). *Levittown: the archetype for suburban development*. HistoryNet. https://www.historynet.com/levittown-the-archetype-for-suburban-development/

77. Hall, P. (2021, June 25). Wall Street crime and punishment: Ivan Boesky gives greed a bad name - Chevron (NYSE:CVX). *Benzinga*. https://www.benzinga.com/news/21/06/21696904/wall-street-crime-and-punishment-ivan-boesky-gives-greed-a-bad-name

78. https://www.benzinga.com/news/21/06/21696904/wall-street-crime-and-punishment-ivan-boesky-gives-greed-a-bad-name

79. Sherman, A. (n.d.). *A Facebook post is on point that Congress is far richer than the American public, but the numbers require more con.* @Politifact. https://www.politifact.com/factchecks/2020/jan/22/facebook-posts/yes-congress-has-disproportionate-share-millionair/

80. Hall, M. (2024, March 21). *Traders have invested $55 million using an app that helps them copy congressional stock portfolios.* Business Insider. https://www.businessinsider.com/more-than-55-million-invested-mimicking-pelosi-crenshaw-trading-portfolios-2024-3

81. Contributor, J. C. O. (2022, July 24). The Hill. *The Hill.* https://thehill.com/opinion/finance/3571790-paul-pelosis-questionable-wall-street-windfall-spurs-bipartisan-calls-for-stock-trading-ban/

82. https://www.opensecrets.org/personal-finances/nancy-pelosi/net-worth?cid=N00007360&year=2018

83. *The Fed - Distribution: Distribution of Household Wealth in the U.S. since 1989.* (n.d.). https://www.federalreserve.gov/releases/z1/dataviz/dfa/distribute/chart/

84. Team, I. (2023, September 1). *Who is David Ricardo and what is he famous for?* Investopedia. https://www.investopedia.com/terms/d/david-ricardo.asp

85. *Private markets: Still waters run deep.* (n.d.). S&P Global. https://www.spglobal.com/en/research-insights/featured/special-editorial/look-forward/private-markets-still-waters-run-deep

86. Chidambaram, P., & Burns, A. (2024, July 9). 10 Things About Long-Term Services and Supports (LTSS) | KFF. KFF. https://www.kff.org/medicaid/issue-brief/10-things-about-long-term-services-and-supports-ltss/

87. Stewart, E. (2020, January 6). What is private equity, and why is it killing everything you love? Vox. https://www.vox.com/the-goods/2020/1/6/21024740/private-equity-taylor-swift-toys-r-us-elizabeth-warren

88. Blasdel, A. (2024, October 10). Slash and burn: is private equity out of control? The Guardian; The Guardian. https://www.theguardian.com/business/2024/oct/10/slash-and-burn-is-private-equity-out-of-control

89. https://www.justice.gov/sites/default/files/nursing_home_staffing_standards_in_state_statutes_and_regulations.pdf

90. Burns, A., Hinton, E., Rudowitz, R., & Mohamed, M. (2025, April 10). 10 things to know about Medicaid | KFF. KFF. https://www.kff.org/medicaid/issue-brief/10-things-to-know-about-medicaid/

91. Alzheimer care home costs - Golden Age Companions. (n.d.). https://www.goldenagecompanions.com/resources/alzheimer-care-home-costs

92. Rafiei, Y. (2022, August 25). When private equity takes over a nursing home. *The New Yorker*. https://www.newyorker.com/news/dispatch/when-private-equity-takes-over-a-nursing-home

93. Johnson, L. (2012b, January 18). Newt Gingrich praised private equity when paid $60,750 to deliver speech. *HuffPost UK*. https://www.huffingtonpost.co.uk/entry/newt-gingrich-private-equity_n_1212980

94. The Curious Case of the $629 Band-Aid | The Takeaway | WNYC Studios. (2017). WNYC Studios. https://www.wnycstudios.org/podcasts/takeaway/segments/how-629-band-aid-explains-american-healthcare

95. Salt in the wound, the cost of healthcare. (2013, August 27). NBC News. https://www.nbcnews.com/id/wbna52852703

96. Petty, C. M. (2023, December 20). What is a private equity firm? ProPublica. https://www.propublica.org/article/what-is-private-equity

97. Waters, C. (2023, February 22). *Wall Street has purchased hundreds of thousands of single-family homes since the Great Recession. Here's what that means for rental prices.* CNBC. https://www.cnbc.com/2023/02/21/how-wall-street-bought-single-family-homes-and-put-them-up-for-rent.html

98. Npr. (2008, September 30). Tom Wolfe on "Masters of the Universe." *NPR*. https://www.npr.org/2008/09/30/95212385/tom-wolfe-on-masters-of-the-universe

99. Chaturvedi, V. (2024, March 27). The biggest financial frauds ever — from Sam Bankman-Fried to Bernie Madoff. *Quartz*. https://qz.com/financial-frauds-sam-bankman-fried-bernie-madoff-enron-1851367680

100. Heakal, R. (2024, January 25). Glass-Steagall Act of 1933: Definition, Effects, and Repeal. Investopedia. https://www.investopedia.com/articles/03/071603.asp

101. Matthew Smith, Danny Yagan, Owen Zidar, Eric Zwick, Capitalists in the Twenty-First Century, The Quarterly Journal of Economics, Volume 134, Issue 4, November 2019, Pages 1675–1745, https://doi.org/10.1093/qje/qjz020

102. Stephens-Davidowitz, S. (2023, January 26). Opinion | The rich are not who we think they are. and happiness is not what we think it is, either. *The New York Times*. https://www.nytimes.com/2022/05/14/opinion/sunday/rich-happiness-big-data.html

103. *IBISWorld - industry market research, reports, and statistics.* (n.d.). https://www.ibisworld.com/united-states/industry-trends/biggest-industries-by-revenue/

104. https://www.nada.org/media/4695/download?inline

105. IBISWorld - industry market research, reports, and statistics. (n.d.). https://www.ibisworld.com/united-states/industry-trends/biggest-industries-by-revenue/

106. Wyman, P. (2021, September 23). Patrick Wyman: Trump and the American Gentry. *The Atlantic*. https://www.theatlantic.com/ideas/archive/2021/09/trump-american-gentry-wyman-elites/620151/

107. Sherman, C. (2024, November 8). 'A big cratering': an expert on gen Z's surprise votes – and young women's growing support for Trump. The Guardian. https://www.theguardian.com/us-news/2024/nov/08/young-voters-trump-gen-z

108. https://crsreports.congress.gov/product/pdf/r/r42346

109. Sherman, E. (2024, August 31). Why Kamala Harris' $25K house down payment plan isn't a disaster. Forbes. https://www.forbes.com/sites/eriksherman/2024/08/31/why-kamala-harriss-25k-house-down-payment-plan-isnt-a-disaster/

110. https://www.dan-wood.co.uk/en/projects/point-114e

111. Ramirez, N. M. (2023, December 11). Politico owner asked execs to pray for Trump's re-election: Report. *Rolling Stone*. https://www.rollingstone.com/politics/politics-news/politico-owner-pray-for-trump-mathias-dopfner-axel-springer-1234587243/

112. Reich, R. (2022, August 24). The changes at CNN look politically motivated. That should concern us all. *The Guardian*. https://www.theguardian.com/commentisfree/2022/aug/24/the-changes-at-cnn-look-politically-motivated-that-should-concern-us-all

113. Henderson, A. (2013, November 15). That's the way it was: Remembering Walter Cronkite. *Smithsonian Magazine.* https://www.smithsonianmag.com/smithsonian-institution/thats -the-way-it-was-remembering-walter-cronkite-16465625/

114. *Walter Cronkite quotes.* (n.d.). BrainyQuote. https://www.brainyquote.com/authors/walte r-cronkite-quotes

115. Johnson, H. (2021, April 29). The unprecedented consolidation of the modern media industry has severe consequences – The Miscellany News. The Miscellany News. https://miscellanynews.org/2021/04/29/opinions/the-unprecedented-consolidatio n-of-the-modern-media-industry-has-severe-consequences/

116. Atske, S. (2024, October 16). News platform fact sheet. Pew Research Center. https://ww w.pewresearch.org/journalism/fact-sheet/news-platform-fact-sheet/

117. Atske, S. (2024, October 16). News platform fact sheet. Pew Research Center. https://ww w.pewresearch.org/journalism/fact-sheet/news-platform-fact-sheet/

118. Castillo, M. (2018, September 10). Les Moonves made more than $650 million as CEO of CBS, and now he could leave with no severance. *CNBC.* https://www.cnbc.com/2018/09/ 10/les-moonves-made-650-million-as-cbs-ceo-could-have-no-severance.html

119. https://www.politico.com/blogs/politico-now/2011/06/jon-stewart-says-press-favors-sensat ionalism-036830

120. Bradley, L. (2018, April 30). It's Political Media vs. Comedians as White House Press Associ- ation Disavows Michelle Wolf. *Vanity Fair.* https://www.vanityfair.com/hollywood/2018/ 04/michelle-wolf-white-house-correspondents-dinner-sarah-huckabee-sanders-smokey-eye

121. https://fair.org/extra/the-fairness-doctrine/

122. Abdelfatah, R. (2023, December 28). Editing Reality (2023). *NPR.* https://www.npr.org/ 2023/12/28/1198908351/throughline-12-28-2023

123. Reporter, G. S. (2021, September 14). Cops: the violent legacy of a TV show that sculpted America's view of police. *The Guardian.* https://www.theguardian.com/tv-and-radio/202 0/jun/11/cops-american-police-tv-show

124. Gramlich, J. (2024, April 24). What the data says about crime in the U.S. Pew Research Cen- ter. https://www.pewresearch.org/short-reads/2024/04/24/what-the-data-says-about-crim e-in-the-us/

125. Section 4: Impartiality - Introduction. (n.d.). https://www.bbc.co.uk/editorialguidelines/g uidelines/impartiality/

126. Stelter, B. (2021, November 16). This infamous Steve Bannon quote is key to understanding America's crazy politics. CNN. https://edition.cnn.com/2021/11/16/media/steve-bannon -reliable-sources

127. Paul, C., & Matthews, M. (2016, July 11). *The Russian*. https://www.rand.org/pubs/persp ectives/PE198.html

128. Sarkis, S. (2019, May 19). This is not equal to that: how false equivalence clouds our judgment. Forbes. https://www.forbes.com/sites/stephaniesarkis/2019/05/19/this-is-not-equal -to-that-how-false-equivalence-clouds-our-judgment/

129. Aratani, L. (2024, May 22). Majority of Americans wrongly believe US is in recession – and most blame Biden. The Guardian. https://www.theguardian.com/us-news/article/2024/m ay/22/poll-economy-recession-biden

130. Sonnenfeld, J. A. (2024, September 6). The truth beneath the economic misinformation. Yale Insights. https://insights.som.yale.edu/insights/the-truth-beneath-the-economic-misi nformation

131. Molloy, P. (2024, September 10). *From rambling to rational: the media's Trump sanewashing problem*. The New Republic. https://newrepublic.com/article/185530/media-criticism-tru mp-sanewashing-problem

132. Molloy, P. (2024, September 2). Downplaying Their Bigotry, The New York Times Describes Book-Banning, Hitler-Quoting Group as "Conservative Moms." Readtpa.com; The Present Age. https://www.readtpa.com/p/downplaying-their-bigotry-the-new

133. Medina, E. (2024, March 6). Mark Robinson wins Republican primary for North Carolina governor. *The New York Times*. https://www.nytimes.com/2024/03/05/us/politics/mark-r obinson-north-carolina-governor.html

134. Bianco, W. (2023, June 24). Op/Ed: Trump's indictment is fair, in line with others accused of violating Espionage Act. The Indianapolis Star; Indianapolis Star. https://eu.indystar.com/story/opinion/2023/06/24/trumps-doj-indictment-under-es pionage-act-consistent-with-other-cases/70344095007/

135. Bailey, C. (2023, June 9). Boxes in the bathroom, boxes on stage: Pictures from Trump charges. BBC News. https://www.bbc.co.uk/news/world-us-canada-65862115

136. Greve, J. E. (2024, March 12). Five key takeaways from the House hearing on Robert Hur's Biden report. The Guardian. https://www.theguardian.com/us-news/2024/mar/12/key-ta keaways-house-hearing-robert-hur-biden-report

137. Green, L. (2022, October 2). Confidence Man review: Maggie Haberman takes down Trump. *The Guardian*. https://www.theguardian.com/books/2022/oct/02/confidence-man-revie w-maggie-haberman-donald-trump

138. Cesca, B. The Bob Cesca interview: Driftglass and Bluegal Day. The Bob Cesca Show | News and Politics Podcast. https://www.bobcesca.com/the-bob-cesca-interview-driftglass-and-bl uegal-day/

139. https://crsreports.congress.gov/product/pdf/R/R46751

140. https://www.marketwatch.com/investing/stock/meta

141. Hayes, A. (2024, January 22). *Biggest companies in the world by market cap*. Investopedia. https://www.investopedia.com/biggest-companies-in-the-world-by-market-cap-5212784

142. Seymour, R. (2022, April 25). The machine always wins: what drives our addiction to social media. *The Guardian*. https://www.theguardian.com/technology/2019/aug/23/social-me dia-addiction-gambling

143. Ali, S. (2021, October 28). The Hill. *The Hill*. https://thehill.com/changing-america/enric hment/arts-culture/578724-5-points-for-anger-1-for-a-like-how-facebooks/

144. Graham, M., & Elias, J. (2021, October 13). How Google's $150 billion advertising business works. CNBC. https://www.cnbc.com/2021/05/18/how-does-google-make-money-advert ising-business-breakdown-.html

145. https://www.theguardian.com/technology/2016/jul/15/how-the-internet-was-invented-19 76-arpa-kahn-cerf

146. *A short history of the Web*. (2024b, February 22). CERN. https://www.home.cern/science/c omputing/birth-web/short-history-web

147. Amnesty International. (2023, October 31). Myanmar: Facebook's systems promoted violence against Rohingya; Meta owes reparations – new re- port. https://www.amnesty.org/en/latest/news/2022/09/myanmar-facebooks-systems-pro moted-violence-against-rohingya-meta-owes-reparations-new-report/

148. Solon, O., & Siddiqui, S. (2017, October 31). Russia-backed Facebook posts "reached 126m Americans" during US election. The Guardian. https://www.theguardian.com/technology /2017/oct/30/facebook-russia-fake-accounts-126-million

149. Michael, C. (2023, November 16). Meta allows Facebook and Instagram ads saying 2020 election was rigged. The Guardian. https://www.theguardian.com/technology/2023/nov/ 15/facebook-ads-2020-election-rigged-stolen-instagram-policy

150. Wendling, M. (2024, August 12). How Musk and Trump put aside their differences. BBC News. https://www.bbc.co.uk/news/articles/cvgd08np9z1o

151. Memon, A., Sharma, S., Mohite, S., & Jain, S. (2018). The role of online social networking on deliberate self-harm and suicidality in adolescents: A systematized review of literature. Indian Journal of Psychiatry, 60(4), 384. https://doi.org/10.4103/psychiatry.indianjpsychiatry_41 4_17

152. Bertuzzi, L., & Bertuzzi, L. (2021, July 7). YouTube's algorithm fuelling harmful content, study says. www.euractiv.com. https://www.euractiv.com/section/disinformation/news/yo utubes-algorithm-fuelling-harmful-content-study-says/

153. Stieg, C. (2019, October 23). How Mark Zuckerberg lets his toddlers use their screen time. *CNBC*. https://www.cnbc.com/2019/10/23/how-mark-zuckerberg-manages-kids-screen-t ime.html

154. Statista. (2024, February 28). *Number of smartphone users worldwide 2014-2029*. https://w ww.statista.com/forecasts/1143723/smartphone-users-in-the-world

155. Statista. (2023, August 25). *Facebook: number of mobile daily active users worldwide 2012-2016*. https://www.statista.com/statistics/346195/facebook-global-mobile-dau/

156. *A quote by Lewis Carroll*. (n.d.). https://www.goodreads.com/quotes/9467-alice-laughed-th ere-s-no-use-trying-she-said-one-can-t

157. *X/Twitter MAU worldwide 2019 | Statista*. (2023, September 13). Statista. https://www.st atista.com/statistics/282087/number-of-monthly-active-twitter-users/

158. https://twitter.com/realDonaldTrump/status/232572505238433794?

159. Fisher, M. (2016, May 13). Donald Trump "pretends to be his own spokesman to boast about himself" | The Independent. *The Independent*. https://www.independent.co.uk/news/world/americas/us-politics/donald-trump-pre tends-to-be-his-own-spokesman-to-boast-about-himself-a7027991.html

160. https://twitter.com/realDonaldTrump/status/266035509162303492

161. https://twitter.com/realdonaldtrump/status/449525268529815552

162. Chantler-Hicks, L. (2024, January 11). TikTok prankster Mizzy: I was wild and reckless, now I want to change. Evening Standard. https://www.standard.co.uk/news/london/mizzy-tikt ok-prankster-prison-release-bacari-bronze-o-garro-london-live-b1131157.html

163. ITV News. (2023, May 25). TikToker "Mizzy" fined after invading family home in London. ITV News. https://www.itv.com/news/london/2023-05-24/tiktoker-fined-after-invading-family-home-and-hit-with-social-media-restrictions

164. Mathers, M. (2023, May 26). TikTok prankster Mizzy arrested on suspicion of breaching court order. *The Independent*. https://www.independent.co.uk/news/uk/crime/tiktok-mizzy-charged-prankster-b2346424.html

165. U.S.C. Title 47 - TELECOMMUNICATIONS. (2020). Govinfo.gov. https://www.govinfo.gov/content/pkg/USCODE-2020-title47/html/USCODE-2020-title47-chap5-subchapII-partI-sec230.htm

166. poweredge-xr7620. (2024). Dell.com. https://www.dell.com/en-us/shop/cty/pdp/spd/poweredge-xr7620/pe_xr7620_16789_vi_vp?configurationid=a57dc38a-28bf-46d3-898f-a6a34c5fcea1

167. Bloomberg - Are you a robot? (2024, January 25). https://www.bloomberg.com/news/articles/2024-01-25/meta-building-new-800-million-ai-focused-data-center-in-indiana

168. Kearney, L. (2024, December 20). US data-center power use could nearly triple by 2028, DOE-backed report says. Reuters. https://www.reuters.com/business/energy/us-data-center-power-use-could-nearly-triple-by-2028-doe-backed-report-says-2024-12-20/

169. O'Brien, I. (2024, September 15). Data center emissions probably 662% higher than big tech claims. Can it keep up the ruse? The Guardian. https://www.theguardian.com/technology/2024/sep/15/data-center-gas-emissions-tech

170. Centers, M. D. (2024, June 3). Global data centers (Asia, Europe, U.S.) - Meta Data Centers. Meta Data Centers. https://datacenters.atmeta.com/all-locations/

171. Luscombe, R. (2024, September 15). Musk says humans can be on Mars in four years. Many laugh, but some see purpose. The Guardian. https://www.theguardian.com/technology/2024/sep/15/musk-humans-live-on-mars-spacex

172. NASA. (2024, January 10). *Hazard: distance from Earth - NASA*. https://www.nasa.gov/hrp/hazard-distance-from-earth/

173. Edwards, C. (2023, August 25). Nasa scientist predicts Elon Musk will die of 'intense poisoning' before he gets to Mars as colony is unr. . . The Sun. https://www.thesun.co.uk/tech/23626009/elon-musk-mars-colony-nasa-opinion-death-radiation/

174. *Comparing the atmospheres of Mars and Earth*. (n.d.). https://www.esa.int/ESA_Multimedia/Images/2018/04/Comparing_the_atmospheres_of_Mars_and_Earth

175. Mars.Nasa.Gov. (n.d.). *Mars Report: Dust storms on Mars*. NASA Mars Exploration. https ://mars.nasa.gov/resources/26555/mars-report-dust-storms-on-mars/

176. Humans to Mars will cost about "Half a trillion dollars" and life support roughly two billion dollars. (2016). In *46th International Conference on Environmental Systems*. https://ntrs.na sa.gov/api/citations/20200000973/downloads/20200000973.pdf

177. Wong, M. (2024, March 18). Elon Musk just added a wrinkle to the AI race. *The Atlantic*. h ttps://www.theatlantic.com/technology/archive/2024/03/xai-grok-open-source-ai/677795/

178. Metz, C., Weise, K., Grant, N., & Isaac, M. (2024, March 4). How Elon Musk and Larry Page's AI debate led to OpenAI and an industry boom. *The New York Times*. https://www.nytim es.com/2023/12/03/technology/ai-openai-musk-page-altman.html

179. Guendelsberger, E. (2019). *On the clock: what low-wage work did to me and how it drives America insane.*
First edition. New York, NY, Little, Brown and Company, Hachette Book Group.

180. Newton, C. (2020, April 1). Amazon's poor treatment of workers is catching up to it during the coronavirus crisis. *The Verge*. https://www.theverge.com/interface/2020/4/1/2120116 2/amazon-delivery-delays-coronavirus-worker-strikes

181. Quoteresearch. (2016, February 1). *Human: A Non-Linear Servo-Mechanism Weighing Only 150 Pounds that Can Be Produced Cheaply by Unskilled Labor – Quote Investigator®*. https: //quoteinvestigator.com/2016/02/01/computer/

182. Vallance, B. S. M. &. C. (2023, October 19). Amazon trials humanoid robots to "free up" staff. *BBC News*. https://www.bbc.co.uk/news/technology-67163680

183. Quoteresearch. (2022, January 30). *The Factory of the Future will have only two employees, a man and a dog – quote Investigator®*. https://quoteinvestigator.com/2022/01/30/future-f actory/

184. U.S. Census Bureau. (2022, July 27). *Number of truckers at All-Time high*. Census.gov. https://www.census.gov/library/stories/2019/06/america-keeps-on-trucking.html

185. How Self-Driving Trucks Really Work I Future Of Work (HBO). (2019). [YouTube Video]. In *YouTube*. https://www.youtube.com/watch?v=Qs69m9T-4Rk

186. VICE News. (2019, September 3). *How Self-Driving Trucks Really Work I Future of Work (HBO)* [Video]. YouTube. https://www.youtube.com/watch?v=Qs69m9T-4Rk

187. https://migway.com/blog/top-10-truck-stops-migways-guide-to-the-best-pit-stops-in-the-us/

188. Listen, liberal, or, What ever happened to the party of the people? Frank, Thomas: Metropolitan Books, 2016.

189. Lhuer, X. (2016, December 6). The next acronym you need to know about: RPA (robotic process automation) | McKinsey. Www.mckinsey.com. https://www.mckinsey.com/capabil ities/mckinsey-digital/our-insights/the-next-acronym-you-need-to-know-about-rpa

190. Yang, A. (2018). *The war on normal people: the truth about America's disappearing jobs and why universal basic income is our future.*
First edition. New York, Hachette Books.

191. *Bloomberg - Are you a robot?* (2017, February 28). https://www.bloomberg.com/news/artic les/2017-02-28/jpmorgan-marshals-an-army-of-developers-to-automate-high-finance

192. Duranton, S. (2024, August 27). Are coders' jobs at risk? AI's impact on the future of programming. Forbes. https://www.forbes.com/sites/sylvainduranton/2024/04/15/are-co ders-jobs-at-risk-ais-impact-on-the-future-of-programming/

193. Kelly, J. (2024, November 1). AI Writes Over 25% Of Code At Google—What Does The Future Look Like For Software Engineers? Forbes. https://www.forbes.com/sites/jackkelly /2024/11/01/ai-code-and-the-future-of-software-engineers/

194. Tai, A. (2022, July 18). I had many conversations with software engineers in various domains and disciplines during the past 20 years of my career as a software engineer and software architect. Some of them were senior engineers having 8 or 10 years of experience. Linkedin.com. https://www.linkedin.com/pulse/what-takes-become-software-architect-alan-tai

195. Weatherbed, J. (2024, August 19). Tesla is hiring people to train its Optimus bot via motion capture. The Verge. https://www.theverge.com/2024/8/19/24223626/tesla-optimus-hum anoid-robot-motion-capture-training

196. Emir, C. (2023, March 3). Tesla Day: 'Optimus' AI robots may outnumber humans in future, claims Elon Musk. *Interesting Engineering*. https://interestingengineering.com/innovation /tesla-optimus-ai-robots-may-outnumber-humans

197. Mahdawi, A. (2024, April 17). The media industry is dying – but I can still get paid to train AI to replace me. The Guardian. https://www.theguardian.com/commentisfree/2024/apr/ 17/the-media-industry-is-dying-but-i-can-still-get-paid-to-train-ai-to-replace-me

198. Forrest, A. (2023, November 3). Elon Musk tells Sunak AI means we won't have to work anymore. *The Independent*. https://www.independent.co.uk/news/uk/politics/rishi-sunak -elon-musk-ai-b2440764.html

199. Forrest, A. (2023, November 3). Elon Musk tells Sunak AI means we won't have to work anymore. *The Independent.* https://www.independent.co.uk/news/uk/politics/rishi-sunak -elon-musk-ai-b2440764.html

200. https://www.facebook.com/entertainmentweekly. (2024). "Face/Off" star Nicolas Cage warns actors that studios will use AI to "change your face." EW.com. https://ew.com/nico- las-cage-warns-actors-that-studios-will-use-ai-to-change-your-face-8731528

201. Metrology News. (2024, August 5). Fully autonomous 'Dark' smart factory runs 24/7. Metrology and Quality News - Online Magazine. https://metrology.news/autonomous-dar k-smart-factory-runs-24-7-without-human-intervention/

202. Goodison, S. (2022). Local Police Departments Personnel, 2020. https://bjs.ojp.gov/sites/g /files/xyckuh236/files/media/document/lpdp20.pdf

203. Greenberg, J. (n.d.). How many police departments are in the US? @Politi- fact. https://www.politifact.com/factchecks/2016/jul/10/charles-ramsey/how-many-polic e-departments-are-us/.

204. Berman, M. (2021, May 9). Most police departments in America are small. That's partly why changing policing is difficult, experts say. Washington Post. https://www.washingtonpost.com/nation/2021/05/08/most-police-departments-am erica-are-small-thats-partly-why-changing-policing-is-difficult-experts-say/

205. Hlr. (2023, March 24). Law Enforcement's "Warrior" Problem. Harvard Law Review. http s://harvardlawreview.org/forum/vol-128/law-enforcements-warrior-problem/

206. Harrell, E., Davis, E., U.S. Department of Justice, & Bureau of Justice Statistics. (2020). Con- tacts between Police and the Public, 2018 – Statistical tables. In Bureau of Justice Statistics. https://bjs.ojp.gov/content/pub/pdf/cbpp18st.pdf.

207. Legalize It All: How to win the war on drugs by Dan Baum: Harper's Magazine April 2016

208. AFP. (2021, April 30). Civil asset forfeiture: seven horror stories - Americans for Prosperity. Americans for Prosperity. https://americansforprosperity.org/blog/civil-asset-forfeiture-ho rror-stories/

209. Swanson, A. (2021, November 25). State police have received billions of dollars of military equipment. Here's where it all went. Washington Post. https://www.washingtonpost.com/news/wonk/wp/2015/04/16/state-police-have-re ceived-billions-of-dollars-of-military-equipment-heres-where-it-all-went/.

210. Wofford, T. (2016, February 26). How America's Police Became an army: The 1033 Program. Newsweek. https://www.newsweek.com/how-americas-police-became-army-1033-program-264537

211. Statistics on Law Enforcement Officer Deaths in the Line of Duty from January through August 2024 | Law Enforcement. (2024). Law Enforcement. https://le.fbi.gov/cjis-division/cjis-link/statistics-on-law-enforcement-officer-deaths-in-the-line-of-duty-from-january-through-august-2024

212. Gramlich, J. (2024, April 24). What the data says about crime in the U.S. Pew Research Center. https://www.pewresearch.org/short-reads/2024/04/24/what-the-data-says-about-crime-in-the-us/

213. Levin, S. (2024, January 8). 2023 saw record killings by US police. Who is most affected? The Guardian. https://www.theguardian.com/us-news/2024/jan/08/2023-us-police-violence-increase-record-deadliest-year-decade

214. Horton, J. (2021, May 17). How US police training compares with the rest of the world. BBC News. https://www.bbc.co.uk/news/world-us-canada-56834733

215. Qualified Immunity FAQ. (n.d.). Legal Defense Fund. https://www.naacpldf.org/qualified-immunity/

216. Opinion pieces | U.S. Representative Don Beyer. (2021, May 24). U.S. Representative Don Beyer. https://beyer.house.gov/news/documentsingle.aspx?DocumentID=5261 .

217. Shoub, K., Christiani, L., Baumgartner, F. R., Epp, D. A., & Roach, K. (2020). Fines, Fees, Forfeitures, and Disparities: A Link Between Municipal Reliance on Fines and Racial Disparities in Policing. Policy Studies Journal, 49(3). https://doi.org/10.1111/psj.12412

218. https://www.vera.org/news/low-level-traffic-stops-are-ineffective-and-sometimes-deadly-why-are-they-still-happening

219. Anderson, M. (2024, August 10). 10 years after Michael Brown's death, police killings are not going down. NPR. https://www.npr.org/2024/08/09/nx-s1-5053165/ferguson-michael-brown-10-years-police

220. Justice Department announces findings of two civil rights investigations in Ferguson, Missouri. (2017, May 23). https://www.justice.gov/opa/pr/justice-department-announces-findings-two-civil-rights-investigations-ferguson-missouri.

221. Inquest, & Farias, C. (2024, August 7). Ferguson at Ten: Ferguson's Pound of Flesh | INQUEST. Inquest. https://inquest.org/fergusons-pound-of-flesh/

222. Brooks, Rosa, Tangled Up in Blue: Policing the American City. New York, Penguin Press, 2021.

223. https://www.vera.org/news/most-911-calls-have-nothing-to-do-with-crime-why-are-we-still -sending-police.

224. Asher, J., & Horwitz, B. (2021, November 8). How do the police actually spend their time? The New York Times. https://www.nytimes.com/2020/06/19/upshot/unrest-police-time -violent-crime.html.

225. Climer, B. A., & Gicker, B. (2021, January 29). CAHOOTS: A Model for Prehospital Mental Health Crisis Intervention. Psychiatric Times. https://www.psychiatrictimes.com/view/cah oots-model-prehospital-mental-health-crisis-intervention

226. Ray, R. (2023, March 16). New Jersey ARRIVE Together program could reform policing as we know it. Brookings. https://www.brookings.edu/research/new-jersey-arrive-together-pr ogram-could-reform-policing-as-we-know-it/.

227.

228. Reporter, G. S. (2018b, March 31). A "hellish world": the mental health crisis overwhelming America's prisons. The Guardian. https://www.theguardian.com/society/2018/mar/31/m ental-health-care-crisis-overwhelming-prison-jail.

229. USAFacts. (2023, March 28). How much do states spend on prisons? USAFacts. https://u safacts.org/articles/how-much-do-states-spend-on-prisons/.

230. Anonymous. (n.d.). The Economic Burden of Incarceration in the U.S (2016). National Institute of Corrections. https://nicic.gov/weblink/economic-burden-incarceration-us-2016.

231. How police unions responded to the assault on the Capitol. (n.d.). Mother Jones. https://www.motherjones.com/2020-elections/2021/01/how-police-unions-respon ded-to-the-assault-on-the-capitol/

232. https://www.huffingtonpost.co.uk/entry/trump-jan-6-police-unions_n_65d67a16e4b0b65 d69218857

233. https://www.ncbi.nlm.nih.gov/pmc/articles/PMC8220482/.

234. PTSD among Police Officers: Impact on Critical Decision Making. (n.d.). https://cops.usd oj.gov/html/dispatch/05-2018/PTSD.html

235. Today, C. S. U. (2022, June 10). Police, firefighters die by suicide more often than in line of duty. Why rates remain high. USA TODAY. https://eu.usatoday.com/story/news/nation/2 022/06/10/high-suicide-rate-police-firefighters-mental-health/7470846001/.

236. Initiative, P. P. (n.d.). United States profile. Prison Policy Initiative. https://www.prisonpol
     icy.org/profiles/US.html

237. Wood, J. (2020, September 19). The US police department that decided to hire social workers.
     The Guardian. https://www.theguardian.com/us-news/2020/sep/19/alexandria-kentucky
     -police-social-workers.

238. https://tvshowtranscripts.ourboard.org/viewtopic.php?f=184&t=39392

239. Wikipedia Contributors. (2019, November 18). Anti-Catholicism in the United States.
     Wikipedia; Wikimedia Foundation. https://en.wikipedia.org/wiki/Anti-Catholicism_in_th
     e_United_States

240. Puzo, M., Coppola, F. F., & Mario Puzo. (n.d.). *THE GODFATHER*. https://www.public
     .asu.edu/~srbeatty/394/Godfather.pdf

241. Marshall, H. (2013). "Come heavy, or not at all." *Journal of Contemporary Criminal Justice*,
     29(2), 276–295. https://doi.org/10.1177/1043986213485619

242. Violent crime is falling nationwide — Here's how we know. (n.d.). Brennan Center for Jus-
     tice. https://www.brennancenter.org/our-work/analysis-opinion/violent-crime-falling-nati
     onwide-heres-how-we-know

243. Bjornstrom EE, Kaufman RL, Peterson RD, Slater MD. RACE AND ETHNIC

244. *In brief: Block by block: Zeroing in on crime Trends | National Institute of Justice*. (n.d.).
     National Institute of Justice. https://nij.ojp.gov/topics/articles/brief-block-block-zeroing-c
     rime-trends

245. Arnade, C. (2017, July 14). White flight followed factory jobs out of Gary, Indiana. Black
     people didn't have a choice. The Guardian. https://www.theguardian.com/society/2017/m
     ar/28/poverty-racism-gary-indiana-factory-jobs

246. US Census Bureau. (2024, April 4). Nation's Urban and Rural Populations Shift Following
     2020 Census. Census.gov. https://www.census.gov/newsroom/press-releases/2022/urban-r
     ural-populations.html

247. Mettler, K. (2018, December 24). What Ronald Reagan actually said about
     border security — according to history, not President Trump. *Washington
     Post*. https://www.washingtonpost.com/politics/2018/12/21/what-ronald-reagan-actually
     -said-about-border-security-according-history-not-donald-trump/

248. Mettler, K. (2018b, December 24). What Ronald Reagan actually said about border security — according to history, not President Trump. *Washington Post*. https://www.washingtonpost.com/politics/2018/12/21/what-ronald-reagan-actually -said-about-border-security-according-history-not-donald-trump/

249. Mettler, K. (2018b, December 24). What Ronald Reagan actually said about border security — according to history, not President Trump. *Washington Post*. https://www.washingtonpost.com/politics/2018/12/21/what-ronald-reagan-actually -said-about-border-security-according-history-not-donald-trump/

250.

251. Palmer, E. (2024, July 18). MAGA makes racist attacks against JD Vance's wife. Newsweek. https://www.newsweek.com/jd-vance-wife-attacks-maga-trump-running-mate-1926194

252. BBC News. (2018, January 15). *Donald Trump denies being a racist after reported crude remark*. https://www.bbc.co.uk/news/world-us-canada-42685356

253. The Bible: Leviticus 19:34

254. Lopez, G. (2014, September 5). 25 years ago, President Bush escalated the war on drugs. Here are the results. Vox. https://www.vox.com/2014/9/5/6106169/george-hw-bush-war-on-dr ugs-25-year-anniversary

255. Gilman, D. (2008). OBSTRUCTING HUMAN RIGHTS: THE TEXAS-MEXICO BORDER WALL The Working Group on Human Rights and the Border Wall. https://l aw.utexas.edu/humanrights/borderwall/analysis/briefing-INTRODUCTION.pdf

256. Linthicum, K. (2018, May 24). There is only one gun store in all of Mexico. So why is gun violence soaring? - Los Angeles Times. *Los Angeles Times*. https://www.latimes.com/world /la-fg-mexico-guns-20180524-story.html

257. Beast, D. (2024, April 13). *The dirty little gun secret behind MAGA World's migrant hysteria*. Apple Podcasts. https://podcasts.apple.com/us/podcast/the-dirty-little-gun-secret-beh ind-maga-worlds/id1508202790?i=1000652371728

258. John. (2023, June 8). *Key facts on U.S.-Sourced guns and violence in Mexico*. Stop US Arms to Mexico. https://stopusarmstomexico.org/key-facts-on-u-s-sourced-guns-and-violence-in-m exico/

259. https://www.congress.gov/bill/109th-congress/senate-bill/397/text

260. Mérancourt, W., & Coletta, A. (2024, April 9). When Haiti's gangs shop for guns, the United States is their store. *Washington Post*. https://www.washingtonpost.com/world/2024/04/0 5/haiti-gangs-american-guns/

261. Thank you to John Fugelsang for this phrase. He has said it many times on his brilliant "Tell Me Everything" show on SiriusXM Insight, Channel 127.

262. https://www.marketwatch.com/story/why-the-fed-has-more-scope-to-let-the-economy-and -job-growth-run-hot-b710f221

263. https://www.nytimes.com/2019/12/31/us/trump-undocumented-workers-winery.html

264. https://edition.cnn.com/2006/POLITICS/03/30/ivins.immigration/

265. Rashid, H. (2024, May 23). Senate Republicans kill their own border deal to suck up to Trump. The New Republic. https://newrepublic.com/post/181896/senate-republicans-ki ll-border-deal-suck-trump

266. O'Connell, O. (2024, February 7). Chip Roy says Trump failed to 'close the border' during every year of his presidency. *The Independent*. https://www.independent.co.uk/news/world /americas/us-politics/trump-close-border-chip-roy-b2492354.html

267. https://x.com/HowardMortman/status/1834221488292929745

268. *How Trump won the unhappiness vote*. (2020, September 18). Stanford HAI. https://hai.sta nford.edu/news/how-trump-won-unhappiness-vote

269. US Census Bureau. (2023, September 12). *Income in the United States: 2022*. Census.gov. https://www.census.gov/library/publications/2023/demo/p60-279.html

270. Schofield H, Venkataramani AS. Poverty-related bandwidth constraints reduce the value of consumption. Proc Natl Acad Sci U S A. 2021 Aug 31;118(35):e2102794118. doi: 10.1073 /pnas.2102794118. PMID: 34446552; PMCID: PMC8536330.

271. Harris, D. (2024, April 15). Is money making you sick? *TIME*. https://time.com/6966650 /money-stress-illness/

272. Light, M. T., He, J., & Robey, J. P. (2020). Comparing crime rates between undocument-ed immigrants, legal immigrants, and native-born US citizens in Texas. Proceedings of the National Academy of Sciences of the United States of America, 117(51), 32340–32347. https://doi.org/10.1073/pnas.2014704117

273. Elizabeth Kolbert, Kirsten Weir, & NLP's Checkology. (2021). Confirmation bias & moti-vated reasoning. In *The New Yorker* [Article]. https://newslit.org/wp-content/uploads/202 2/07/InBrief-ConfirmationBiasMotivatedReasoning-FINAL.pdf

274. https://www.nytimes.com/2016/12/21/upshot/the-long-term-jobs-killer-is-not-chi-na-its-automation.html

275. Banks, J. (2024, April 8). *Why you can't think straight when you're stressed.* https://www.lin kedin.com/pulse/why-you-cant-think-straight-when-youre-stressed-jo-banks

276. Jardine, L. (2012, September 20). Lyndon B Johnson: The uncivil rights reformer. The Independent. https://www.independent.co.uk/news/presidents/lyndon-b-johnson-the-un civil-rights-reformer-1451816.html

277. Mayer, J. (2016, August 15). LBJ Fights the White Backlash. National Archives. https://w ww.archives.gov/publications/prologue/2001/spring/lbj-and-white-backlash-1

278. Emery, D. (2016, August 23). *Did Lyndon B. Johnson say this about the "Lowest White Man" and "Best Colored Man"?* Snopes. https://www.snopes.com/fact-check/lbj-convince-the-lo west-white-man/

279. 'The writing was on the wall' – Ash Center. (2024, November 13). Ash Center. https://ash .harvard.edu/articles/the-writing-was-on-the-wall/

280. Grabar, H. (2024, November 14). The new Trump voters no one wants to talk about. Slate Magazine. https://slate.com/business/2024/11/trump-shift-blue-cities-latino-minority-vot e-news-source-tiktok-mainstream-media.html

281. Reporter, G. S. (2024a, September 26). TikTok videos spread misinformation to new migrant community in New York City. The Guardian. https://www.theguardian.com/technology/ 2024/sep/26/tiktok-misinformation-migrants-new-york-city

282. The Race-Class Narrative Project | Demos. (n.d.). Demos. https://www.demos.org/campai gn/race-class-narrative-project

283. Greater than fear: Winning progressive change in Minnesota - the Shorty Awards. (n.d.). https://shortyawards.com/11th/greater-than-fear-winning-progressive-change-in-minnesota

284. Moms for Liberty Loves DeSantis—but They'll Never Vote for Him. (2023, July 7). Apple Podcasts. https://podcasts.apple.com/us/podcast/moms-for-liberty-loves-desantis-but-they ll-never-vote/id1508202790?i=1000619734776

285. The 4 Strongest Predictors of Divorce. (2024). Psychology Today. https://www.psychology today.com/gb/blog/social-instincts/202409/the-4-strongest-predictors-of-divorce

286. *Self-Determination Theory of Motivation - Center for Community Health & Prevention - University of Rochester Medical Center.* (n.d.). https://www.urmc.rochester.edu/commun ity-health/patient-care/self-determination-theory.aspx

287. Watson, S. (2024, April 18). Dopamine: the Pathway to Pleasure. Harvard Health; Harvard Medical School. https://www.health.harvard.edu/mind-and-mood/dopamine-the-pathway -to-pleasure

288. Rodriguez, G. R. (2017, July 24). This is your brain on storytelling: the chemistry of modern communication. Forbes. https://www.forbes.com/sites/giovannirodriguez/2017/07/21/this-is-your-brain-on-storytelling-the-chemistry-of-modern-communication/?sh=27bb3e7dc865

289. Campus Recreation | Nature's Painkiller: How Endorphins Play A Significant Role In Exercise. (2020, July 6). Wvu.edu. https://campusrecreation.wvu.edu/news-and-events/archive/2020/07/06/natures-pain-killer-how-endorphins-play-a-significant-role-in-exercise

290. Exercising to relax. (2020, July 7). Harvard Health; Harvard Health Publishing. https://www.health.harvard.edu/staying-healthy/exercising-to-relax

291. TEDx Talks. (2017, March 16). The magical science of storytelling | David JP Phillips | TEDxStockholm [Video]. YouTube. https://www.youtube.com/watch?v=Nj-hdQMa3uA

292. https://www.ncbi.nlm.nih.gov/pmc/articles/PMC4449495/

293. Vietnam War Statistics. (n.d.). Www.vva310.org. https://www.vva310.org/vietnam-war-statistics

294. The Editors of Encyclopaedia Britannica. (n.d.). Who won the Vietnam War? | Britannica. Encyclopedia Britannica. https://www.britannica.com/question/Who-won-the-Vietnam-War

295. Vietnam: Welcome Home. Iowapbs.org. https://www.iowapbs.org/iowapathways/artifact/1599/vietnam-welcome-home

296. Vietnam War Statistics. (n.d.). Www.vva310.org. https://www.vva310.org/vietnam-war-statistics

297. https://www.ncbi.nlm.nih.gov/pmc/articles/PMC5371751/

298. Janos, A., & Janos, A. (2018, August 29). *G.I.s' drug use in Vietnam Soared—With their commanders' help*. HISTORY. https://www.history.com/news/drug-use-in-vietnam

299. Spiegel, A. (2012, January 2). What Vietnam taught us about breaking bad habits. *NPR*. https://www.npr.org/sections/health-shots/2012/01/02/144431794/what-vietnam-taught-us-about-breaking-bad-habits

300. Gerretsen, I. (2023, May 9). *Is there such a thing as an addictive personality?* https://www.bbc.com/future/article/20230505-is-there-such-a-thing-as-an-addictive-personality

301. Youth Forward. (2023, January 31). *The Answer is Rat Park*. https://www.youth-forward.org/the-answer-is-rat-park/

302. Linné, T. (2023, December 4). Rats are more human than you think – and they certainly like being around us. The Conversation. https://theconversation.com/rats-are-more-human-th an-you-think-and-they-certainly-like-being-around-us-216846

303. FastStats. (n.d.). Inpatient Surgery. https://www.cdc.gov/nchs/fastats/inpatient-surgery.htm

304. *Relative analgesic potency of intramuscular heroin and morphine in cancer patients with post-operative pain and chronic pain due to cancer.* (1981, February 1). PubMed. https://pubmed .ncbi.nlm.nih.gov/6783935/

305. Di Justo, P. (2011, January 31). What's inside: street heroin. WIRED. https://www.wired.c om/2011/01/st-whatsinside-heroin/

306. Hall, W., & Weier, M. (2016). Lee Robins' studies of heroin use among US Vietnam veterans. *Addiction*, *112*(1), 176–180. https://doi.org/10.1111/add.13584

307. *Fentanyl DrugFacts | National Institute on Drug Abuse.* (2023, March 3). National Institute on Drug Abuse. https://nida.nih.gov/publications/drugfacts/fentanyl

308. Cuddihy, C. (2019, January 8). More coal power plant shutdowns under Trump than Obama. *World Coal.* https://www.worldcoal.com/power/08012019/more-coal-power-plant-shutd owns-under-trump-than-obama/

309. *Topic: Coal mining in the U.S.* (2024, August 8). Statista. https://www.statista.com/topics/ 5165/coal-mining-in-the-us/

310. https://www.epa.gov/ghgemissions/sources-greenhouse-gas-emissions

311. *Frequently asked questions (FAQs) - U.S. Energy Information Administration (EIA).* (n.d.). https://www.eia.gov/tools/faqs/faq.php?id=65&t=21

312. *GHGRP Power Plants | US EPA.* (2024, March 11). US EPA. https://www.epa.gov/ghgrep orting/ghgrp-power-plants

313. Butterworth, P. (2023, March 20). Carbon capture economics: Why $200/tCO2 is the crucial figure. CRU Group Website. https://sustainability.crugroup.com/article/carbon-capture-e conomics-why-usd-200-per-tco2-is-the-crucial-figure

314. As carbon air capture ramps up, major hurdles remain. (n.d.). Yale E360. https://e360.yale.e du/features/direct-air-capture

315. Carbon capture and storage in the United States. (2023, December 1). Congressional Budget Office. https://www.cbo.gov/publication/59832

316. Gammon, K. (2023, November 22). Suck carbon from the air? US facility launches novel climate solution. The Guardian. https://www.theguardian.com/environment/2023/nov/19/carbon-dioxide-direct-air-capture

317. Carrington, D. (2023, January 24). 'No miracles needed': Prof Mark Jacobson on how wind, sun and water can power the world. *The Guardian*. https://www.theguardian.com/environment/2023/jan/23/no-miracles-needed-prof-mark-jacobson-on-how-wind-sun-and-water-can-power-the-world

318. *Nuclear*. (n.d.). Energy.gov. https://www.energy.gov/nuclear

319. Lelieveld, J., Haines, A., Burnett, R. T., Tonne, C., Klingmüller, K., Münzel, T., & Pozzer, A. (2023). Air pollution deaths attributable to fossil fuels: observational and modelling study. BMJ, e077784. https://doi.org/10.1136/bmj-2023-077784

320. Amy, J. (2023, December 19). 2 nuclear reactors that can power 1 million US homes with clean, sustainable energy is $21 billion over budget and years behind schedule. *Business Insider*. https://www.businessinsider.com/georgia-nuclear-reactors-billions-over-budget-years-behind-schedule-2023-12

321. *Jobs*. (n.d.). Nuclear Energy Institute. https://www.nei.org/advantages/jobs

322. Pener, D. (2022, November 8). Billy Ray, Gregg Hurwitz discuss messaging advice they offered dozens of Democratic candidates this year. The Hollywood Reporter. https://www.hollywoodreporter.com/news/politics-news/movie-book-writers-democrats-advice-elections-2022-1235258130/

323. https://pubs.usgs.gov/periodicals/mcs2024/mcs2024-soda-ash.pdf

324. Wainwright, O. (2023, May 23). How solar farms took over the California desert: 'An oasis has become a dead sea.' *The Guardian*. https://www.theguardian.com/us-news/2023/may/21/solar-farms-energy-power-california-mojave-desert

325. U.S. Census Bureau. (2021, October 8). Latest city and town population estimates of the decade show Three-Fourths of the nation's incorporated places have fewer than 5,000 people. Census.gov. https://www.census.gov/library/stories/2020/05/america-a-nation-of-small-towns.html

326. Milman, O., & Witherspoon, A. (2024, January 26). The US says it needs up to 22m acres for the solar energy transition – here's what that looks like. The Guardian. https://www.theguardian.com/us-news/2024/jan/23/us-solar-energy-transition-land

327. U.S. farming: total land in farms 2023 | Statista. (2024, May 24). Statista. https://www.statista.com/statistics/196104/total-area-of-land-in-farms-in-the-us-since-2000/

328. https://emp.lbl.gov/utility-scale-solar

329. *Gas mileage of All-Electric vehicles*. (n.d.). https://www.fueleconomy.gov/feg/byfuel/EV20 22.shtml

330. Mihalascu, D. (2023, November 19). 2022 Ford F-150 Lightning: Range, costs, pros and cons at 15,000 miles. *InsideEVs*. https://insideevs.com/news/696737/2022-ford-f-150-lightning -range-costs-pros-cons-15000-miles/

331. https://www.bbc.com/future/article/20230525-how-more-us-female-electricians-helps-climate-change

332. Rowlands, D., & Love, H. (2021, September 28). Mapping rural America's diversity and demographic change. Brookings. https://www.brookings.edu/articles/mapping-rural-americas-diversity-and-demographic-change/

333. Bump, P. (2021, October 23). By 2040, two-thirds of Americans will be represented by 30 percent of the Senate. *Washington Post*. https://www.washingtonpost.com/news/politics/wp/2017/11/28/by-2040-two-thirds-of-americans-will-be-represented-by-30-percent-of-the-senate/

334. *Major party competition in state legislative elections, 2022 - Ballotpedia*. (n.d.). Ballotpedia. https://ballotpedia.org/Major_party_competition_in_state_legislative_elections,_2022

335. *Election results, 2022: Uncontested races by state - Ballotpedia*. (n.d.). Ballotpedia. https://ballotpedia.org/Election_results,_2022:_Uncontested_races_by_state

336. Apple Podcasts. (2024, April 4). *On Democracy with FPWellman on Apple Podcasts*. https://podcasts.apple.com/us/podcast/dirt-road-democrats-need-us-with-jess-piper/id1623863298

337. The Heartland Collective. (2023b, September 14). Dirt Road Democrat - 9/12/23 | Some Kind Of Blue: Meet Michele Hornish, founder of Blue Missouri. [Video]. YouTube. https://www.youtube.com/watch?v=lwF-Og2Kh4E

338. *Rural Democrat: Jess Piper — Future Hindsight*. (2024b, March 15). Future Hindsight. https://www.futurehindsight.com/episodes/rural-democrat-jess-piper

339. *Amazon.com : F Biden and F You for Voting for him! 3x5 Outdoor Double Sided Flag, Anti Joe Biden Flag Banner Vivid Color and UV Fade Resistant, Brass Grommets (Black) : Patio, Lawn & Garden*. (n.d.-b). https://www.amazon.com/Voting-Outdoor-Double-Resistant-Grommets/dp/B08SW9B9DT?th=1

340. Moore, M. (2022, December 30). Blue Dots in a Red Sea (Ep. 5). Michael Moore. https://www.michaelmoore.com/p/blue-dot-tsunami-ep5

341. Kaufman, A. C. (n.d.-d). *Michael Bloomberg has a toxic legacy on lead*. Mother Jones. https://www.motherjones.com/environment/2019/12/michael-bloomberg-has-a-toxic-legacy-on-lead/

342. *Reclaiming Rural Power: Chloe Maxmin & Canyon Woodward — Future Hindsight*. (2023, April 28). Future Hindsight. https://www.futurehindsight.com/episodes/reclaiming-rural-power-chloe-maxmin-canyon-woodward

343. Contributor, L. J. D. O. (2022b, January 13). The Hill. *The Hill*. https://thehill.com/opinion/campaign/589663-to-progressive-democrats-follow-the-lesson-of-maine-state-sen-chloe-maxmin/

344. https://bioneers.org/how-a-green-new-deal-in-maine-could-transform-progressive-organizing-throughout-the-country-zmbz1904/

345. EcoWatch. (2021e, December 9). Green New Deal champion Chloe Maxmin unseats powerful GOP incumbent in rural Maine. *EcoWatch*. https://www.ecowatch.com/chloe-maxmin-2648658756.html

346. *Maine State Senate District 13 - Ballotpedia*. (n.d.-d). Ballotpedia. https://ballotpedia.org/Maine_State_Senate_District_13

347. https://slate.com/news-and-politics/2020/11/why-susan-collins-won.html

348. Sara Gideon concedes to Susan Collins, dealing a blow to Democratic hopes of regaining Senate. (2020c, November 4). *Salon*. https://www.salon.com/2020/11/04/sara-gideon-concedes-to-susan-collins-dealing-a-blow-to-democratic-hopes-of-regaining-senate/

349. https://mainernews.com/how-sara-gideon-lost-to-collins-the-day-after-she-entered-the-race

350. Why are 600+ rural hospitals at risk of closing? (2023g, March 22). https://www.advisory.com/daily-briefing/2023/03/22/rural-hospitals

351. Gringlas, S. (2024, February 21). Red states that have resisted Medicaid expansion are feeling pressure to give up. NPR. https://www.npr.org/2024/02/21/1232859171/red-states-that-have-resisted-medicaid-expansion-are-feeling-pressure-to-give-up

352. *Why are 600+ rural hospitals at risk of closing?* (2023g, March 22). https://www.advisory.com/daily-briefing/2023/03/22/rural-hospitals

353. Munch, D. (2024, March 7). Over 140,000 Farms Lost in 5 Years. American Farm Bureau Federation. https://www.fb.org/market-intel/over-140-000-farms-lost-in-5-years

354. Murillo-Williams, A. (n.d.). Why we need to keep talking about farm stress. https://extension.psu.edu/why-we-need-to-keep-talking-about-farm-stress

355. Zimmerman, S. (2024, October 24). Big Ag is spending big on lobbying and the 2024 election. Agriculture Dive. https://www.agriculturedive.com/news/agriculture-lobbying-2024-electi on-campaign-spending-farm-bill/730813/

356. McGreal, C. (2019, March 10). How America's food giants swallowed the family farms. The Guardian; The Guardian. https://www.theguardian.com/environment/2019/mar/09/ame rican-food-giants-swallow-the-family-farms-iowa

357. Higgins, J. (2024, August 14). "Land Rich, Cash Poor" looks at America's agriculture crisis through one family farm. Journal Sentinel; Milwaukee Journal Sentinel. https://eu.jsonline.com/story/life/be-wisconsin/2024/08/14/land-rich-cash-poor-bri an-reisinger-review/74704658007/

358. The number of U.S. farms continues slow decline. (n.d.). https://www.ers.usda.gov/data-p roducts/chart-gallery/gallery/chart-detail/?chartId=58268

359. Otte, J. (2024, December 13). "What a circus": eligible US voters on why they didn't vote in the 2024 presidential election. The Guardian; The Guardian. https://www.theguardian.co m/us-news/2024/dec/13/why-eligible-voters-did-not-vote

360. Livingstone, K. (2021, February 9). *Nonvoters 2020: Counted out - Medill News Service*. Medill News Service. https://dc.medill.northwestern.edu/blog/2020/12/15/nonvoters-2020-coun ted-out/#sthash.nqLV1Iqe.dpbs

361. Knight Foundation. (n.d.). The 100 million project. https://knightfoundation.org/reports /the-100-million-project/

362. Wikipedia contributors. (2023, December 24). *Personal income in the United States*. Wikipedia. https://en.wikipedia.org/wiki/Personal_income_in_the_United_States

363. Fíonta, & Fíonta. (2023, July 24). *Which age groups bear the largest share of the tax burden?* Tax Foundation. https://taxfoundation.org/blog/which-age-groups-bear-largest-share -tax-burden/

364. *Update: Three rounds of stimulus checks. See how many went out and for how much.* (2023, November 6). Pandemic Oversight. https://www.pandemicoversight.gov/data-interactive-t ools/data-stories/update-three-rounds-stimulus-checks-see-how-many-went-out-and

365. Nova, A. (2022, June 22). How likely are stimulus checks to be used in the next recession? Economists weigh in. *CNBC*. https://www.cnbc.com/2022/06/22/stimulus-checks-could -be-used-in-the-next-recession-economists-say.html

366. Christopher, T., & Christopher, T. (2023, November 17). *Chris Wallace Charlamagne: Why Trump gaining w Black people?* Mediaite. https://www.mediaite.com/news/cnns-chris-wallace-asks-charlamagne-tha-god-why-trump-gaining-with-black-people-how-do-you-explain-that/

367. Fung, K. (2024a, February 1). Biden sending more direct payments to Americans is worrying Republicans. *Newsweek*. https://www.newsweek.com/biden-sending-more-direct-payments-americans-worrying-republicans-1865980

368. News, P. (2024, December 10). WATCH: Biden looks back at his economic record in speech at Brookings Institution. PBS News. https://www.pbs.org/newshour/politics/watch-live-biden-speaks-on-the-economy-at-the-brookings-institution

369. Vox. (2024, March 11). *Charlamagne tha God on Biden v. Trump*. Apple Podcasts. https://podcasts.apple.com/us/podcast/charlamagne-tha-god-on-biden-v-trump/id1346207297?i=1000648809780

370. Groves, S. (2023, October 20). Republicans are facing death threats as the election for speaker gets mired in personal feuds | AP News. *AP News*. https://apnews.com/article/house-speaker-jim-jordan-threats-54eeecef0188edfcb9903e45019f190f

371. *Citizens United explained*. (2025, January 14). Brennan Center for Justice. https://www.brennancenter.org/our-work/research-reports/citizens-united-explained

372. Reporter, G. S. (2024, November 12). Elon Musk's Super Pac spent $200m to help elect Donald Trump. The Guardian. https://www.theguardian.com/us-news/2024/nov/12/elon-musk-america-pac-donald-trump-campaign

373. Confino, P. (2024, November 9). Reclusive billionaire heir Timothy Mellon gave $125 million to help elect Trump, even more than Elon Musk. Fortune. https://fortune.com/2024/11/09/timothy-mellon-net-worth-top-donor-trump-campaign-elon-musk/

374. Debusmann, B., Jr. (2024, June 3). The billionaires rallying behind Trump after his conviction. BBC News. https://www.bbc.co.uk/news/articles/ckvvlv3lewxo

375. The Democrats will keep losing until they solve their plutocracy problem | The nation. (2025, January 3). The Nation. https://www.thenation.com/article/politics/democrats-donors-plutocracy-problem/

376. https://www.indeed.com/career-advice/pay-salary/army-salary

377. : How Everything Became War and the Military Became Everything, Rosa Brooks. Publisher: Simon & Schuster (July 25, 2017). Length: 448 pages. ISBN13: 9781476777870

378. #158: Navigating Both Sides Of The Aisle - Representative Jason Crow (CO-6). (2025, March 11). Green Beret Foundation. https://greenberetfoundation.org/jedburghpodcast/158-all-or-nothing-wont-work-representative-jason-crow-co-6

379. Marathon Studios Enterprises. (n.d.). E-1 Private Salary - Marine Corps Pay 2024. Military-Ranks.org. https://www.military-ranks.org/marine-corps/private-pay#google_vignette

380. U.S. Department of Defense. (n.d.-a). *DOD reduces On-Base child care fees for military families.* https://www.defense.gov/News/News-Stories/Article/Article/3662171/dod-reduces-on-base-child-care-fees-for-military-families/

381. Podcasts, E. (2022, March 1). *Josh Remillard: Defeating Madison Cawthorn in NC-13.* Evergreen Podcasts. https://evergreenpodcasts.com/burn-the-boats/josh-remillard-defeating-madison-cawthorn-in-nc-13

382. https://www.nytimes.com/2023/10/10/us/schools-pandemic-defense-department.html

383. *M249 Squad Automatic Weapon.* (n.d.). Military.com. https://www.military.com/equipment/m249-squad-automatic-weapon

384. Bushatz, A. (2020, April 21). Can you carry a gun on a military base? *Military.com.* https://www.military.com/pcs/can-you-carry-gun-military-base.html

385. Department of Education releases new data showing the American Rescue Plan and other pandemic relief funds kept millions of college students enrolled in school | U.S. Department of Education. (n.d.). https://www.ed.gov/news/press-releases/department-education-releases-new-data-showing-american-rescue-plan-and-other-pandemic-relief-funds-kept-millions-college-students-enrolled-school

386. https://www.usnews.com/best-colleges/rankings/highest-grad-rate

387. OEDb.org. (2022, July 7). *Schools ranked by graduation rate | OEDB.* OEDB.org. https://www.oedb.org/rankings/graduation-rate/page/6/#table-rankings

388. McNair, K. (2024, May 12). A Harvard education costs over $82,000 a year—here's how much students actually pay. CNBC. https://www.cnbc.com/2024/05/12/how-much-harvard-students-actually-pay-to-attend.html

389. National Center for Education Statistics. (n.d.). *Fast Facts: Endowments (73).* https://nces.ed.gov/fastfacts/display.asp?id=73

390. https://www.usnews.com/education/best-colleges/the-short-list-college/articles/10-universities-with-the-biggest-endowments

391. https://dealbreaker.com/2018/04/john-paulson-singlehandedly-paying-for-trump-tax-cuts

392. Reporter, G. S. (2017, July 14). Hedge fund boss John Paulson gives a record $400m donation to Harvard. *The Guardian*. https://www.theguardian.com/business/2015/jun/04/hedge-f und-boss-john-paulson-gives-a-record-400m-donation-to-harvard

393. Billionaire megadonor Ken Griffin says he will stop donations to Harvard | News | The Harvard Crimson. (n.d.). https://www.thecrimson.com/article/2024/1/31/ken-griffin-pau sing-harvard-donations/

394. Hiltzik, M. (2016, February 24). The rich get richer: Should the wealthy get a tax break for endowing elite universities? - Los Angeles Times. Los Angeles Times. https://www.latimes.com/business/hiltzik/la-fi-mh-should-big-donors-get-a-tax-br eak-universities-20160224-column.html

395. Muniz, H. (n.d.). *The 12 best universities in Canada*. https://blog.prepscholar.com/best-u niversities-in-canada

396. *Tax Ivy League endowments, and fund public higher ed*. (2024, February 26). https://jacobi n.com/2024/02/tax-ivy-league-endowments-public-university-massachusetts

397. Mtadmin. (2024, August 9). Timeline. Harvard University. https://www.harvard.edu/abou t/history/timeline/

398. https://edition.cnn.com/ALLPOLITICS/stories/1999/11/09/trump.rich/index.html

399. https://www.cbo.gov/system/files/2024-02/59710-Outlook-2024.pdf

400. Cassella, M. (2023, October 20). Jerome Powell speech today: Fed chair lays groundwork for holding rates steady; Climate protestors interrupt event. *Bar-rons*. https://www.barrons.com/livecoverage/fed-jerome-powell-speech-today/card/powell -u-s-s-fiscal-path-is-unsustainable--aj3ql5Mct31pIsmCkcYz

401. Fiscal data explains federal spending. (n.d.). https://fiscaldata.treasury.gov/americas-finance -guide/federal-spending/

402. Washington, K. (2024, April 16). *2023-2024 tax brackets and federal income tax rates*. Forbes Advisor. https://www.forbes.com/advisor/taxes/taxes-federal-income-tax-bracket/

403. Haden, J. (2011, December 7). How would you feel about a 94% tax rate? *CBS News*. https ://www.cbsnews.com/news/how-would-you-feel-about-a-94-tax-rate/

404. News, A. (2012, January 18). From Eisenhower to Obama: What the Wealthiest Americans Pay in Taxes. ABC News. https://abcnews.go.com/Politics/eisenhower-obama-wealthy-am ericans-mitt-romney-pay-taxes/story?id=15387862

405. TRADING ECONOMICS. (n.d.). *United States federal corporate tax rate.* https://trading economics.com/united-states/corporate-tax-rate

406. https://www.americanprogress.org/article/these-19-fortune-100-companies-paid-next-to-no thing-or-nothing-at-all-in-taxes-in-2021/

407. Marr, C. (2024, June 24). Record Stock Buybacks Bolster Case for Raising Corporate Tax Rate | Center on Budget and Policy Priorities. Center on Budget and Policy Priorities. http s://www.cbpp.org/blog/record-stock-buybacks-bolster-case-for-raising-corporate-tax-rate

408. Walter, J. R. (2006, January 2). The 3-6-3 Rule: An Urban Myth? Richmondfed.org; Economic Quarterly. https://www.richmondfed.org/publications/research/economic_quarterl y/2006/winter/walter

409. Bloomberg - Are you a robot? (n.d.). https://www.bloomberg.com/billionaires/profiles/wi lliam-h-gates/

410. Tax Foundation. (2024, February 22). Historical income tax Rates and Brackets, 1862-2021. https://taxfoundation.org/data/all/federal/historical-income-tax-rates-brackets/

411. Huddleston, T., Jr. (2020, January 7). Bill Gates: Tax rates on the wealthy were nearly double when we started Microsoft and "it didn't hurt" us. *CNBC.* https://www.cnbc.com/2020/0 1/06/bill-gates-high-taxes-didnt-discourage-him-from-launching-microsoft.html

412. Balara, V. (2019, January 24). Fox News Poll: Voters favor taxing the wealthy, increasing domestic spending. *Fox News.* https://www.foxnews.com/politics/fox-news-poll-voters-fav or-taxing-the-wealthy-increasing-domestic-spending

413. Frank, R. (2024, March 28). The wealth of the 1% just hit a record $44 trillion. CNBC. https://www.cnbc.com/2024/03/28/wealth-of-the-1percent-hits-a-record-44-trillion.html

414. *Top Wealth in America: New Estimates under Heterogeneous Returns - Princeton University - Department of Economics.* (2023, April 19). Princeton University - Department of Economics. https://economics.princeton.edu/working-papers/top-wealth-in-america-new-estimate s-under-heterogenous-returns/#

415. USA Wealth Report 2024. (n.d.). Henley & Partners. https://www.henleyglobal.com/news room/press-releases/usa-wealth-report-2024

416. Feudalism ...alias American Capitalism: A study of American Feudalism in action: David C. French

417. Randall, S. (2024, December 6). What's making America's billionaires richer, faster? Invest mentnews.com; InvestmentNews. https://www.investmentnews.com/ria-news/whats-mak ing-americas-billionaires-richer-faster/258509

418. World Bank Open Data. (n.d.). World Bank Open Data. https://data.worldbank.org/indica tor/NY.GDP.MKTP.CD

419. Rae, D. (2024, February 20). How the rich use the buy, borrow die strategy to avoid large tax bills. *Forbes.* https://www.forbes.com/sites/davidrae/2022/07/14/how-the-rich-use-the-bu y-borrow-die-strategy-to-avoid-large-tax-bills/

420. Bloomberg. (2024, December 11). Elon Musk's net worth tops $400 billion, a historic first. Fortune. https://fortune.com/2024/12/11/elon-musk-net-worth-tops-400-billion-historic -first-richest-man-alive-spacex-tesla/

421. *The Fed - Distribution: Distribution of Household Wealth in the U.S. since 1989.* (n.d.). http s://www.federalreserve.gov/releases/z1/dataviz/dfa/distribute/chart/

422. Fíonta, & Fíonta. (2024, March 5). *A Property Tax is a Wealth Tax, but. . ..* Tax Foundation. https://taxfoundation.org/blog/property-tax-wealth-tax/

423. Tax Foundation. (2024, February 23). *Property tax | TaxEDU Glossary.* https://taxfoundat ion.org/taxedu/glossary/property-tax/

424. Lee, J. (2023, August 17). Here's why Americans can't stop living paycheck to paycheck. *CNBC.* https://www.cnbc.com/2023/08/17/heres-why-americans-cant-stop-living-payche ck-to-paycheck.html

425. White House, CBO, New America, Washington Post, KFF, Treasury, & Joint Committee on Taxation. (n.d.). *PRESIDENT BIDEN'S BUILD BACK BETTER PLAN lowers costs for families and is fully paid for.* https://americansfortaxfairness.org/wp-content/uploads/Fact -Sheet-Nov-2021-COMPLETE-FINAL.pdf

426. *Section 1: Cost of Health Insurance - 10240 | KFF.* (2023, December 8). KFF. https://www.kf f.org/report-section/ehbs-2023-section-1-cost-of-health-insurance/

427. *NHE Fact Sheet | CMS.* (n.d.). https://www.cms.gov/data-research/statistics-trends-and-re ports/national-health-expenditure-data/nhe-fact-sheet

428. https://www.medicaid.gov/medicaid/program-information/medicaid-and-chip-enrollment -data/report-highlights/index.html

429. Mshepard. (2023, June 29). *Medicare enrollment numbers.* Center for Medicare Advocacy. https://medicareadvocacy.org/medicare-enrollment-numbers/

430. Kelly, A. (2024, February 28). Millions of veterans are about to get expanded healthcare access. *Business Insider.* https://www.businessinsider.com/healthcare-for-veterans-expands-toxins -harzards-pact-act-va-2024-2

431. *NHE Fact Sheet | CMS*. (n.d.-b). https://www.cms.gov/data-research/statistics-trends-and-r eports/national-health-expenditure-data/nhe-fact-sheet

432. Congressional Budget Office scores Medicare-For-All: universal coverage for less spending. (2021). [Dataset]. In *Forefront Group*. https://doi.org/10.1377/forefront.20210210.190243